THE STARSKY AND HUTCH TRIVIA QUIZ BOOK

THE STARSKY AND HUTCH TRIVIA QUIZ BOOK

BY

CRISTOPHER DEROSE

BearManor Media

2022

THE STARSKY AND HUTCH TRIVIA QUIZ BOOK

© 2022 *CRISTOPHER DEROSE*

All rights reserved.

Published in the United States of America by:

BearManor Media

4700 Millenia Blvd.
Suite 175 PMB 90497
Orlando, FL 32839

bearmanormedia.com

Printed in the United States.

Typesetting and layout by BearManor Media

ISBN—978-1-62933-884-2

To PMG and DS, who helped a boy see heroes in the real world rather than only beyond the stars.

ZEBRA THREE, COME IN, PLEASE.

In the days of phone booths and no seatbelt laws, the fictional locale of Bay City, Los Angeles was protected by not only uniformed police officers, but those who would operate as plainclothes detectives, going undercover if needed to bring the bad guys in off the streets. Two of them were Detective Sergeants David Starsky and his partner, Kenneth "Hutch" Hutchinson. Together they made the world of Bay City a little safer each week from April 30th, 1975 to May 15th, 1979. Following the pilot, 92 episodes were made over four seasons starring Paul Michael Glaser and David Soul, respectively.

Originally created by William Blinn (1937-2020) who had penned episodes for shows like *Rawhide* and *Gunsmoke* before going on to win Emmy and Peabody Awards for 1971's *Brian's Song*, and he would earn another Emmy for his writing on the TV adaptation for Alex Haley's bestselling novel *Roots*. He would continue to write for *The Rookies, Fame,* and the hit Prince film, *Purple Rain*.

Starsky and Hutch came from Blinn's original idea for a television pilot entitled *Nightside,* involving a pair of cops who worked the night shift. The cost of night shoots proved too big a hurdle for production and the idea was shelved for a few years until it became a pilot known as *Starsky and Hutch* for Spelling-Goldberg Productions.

The pilot went to series and was a veritable hit, with the first episode, "Savage Sunday" finishing at #16 and 22.6 share in the AC Nielsen ratings. But viewers were unaware that two real-life NYPD officers, Lou Telano and John Sepe, who served in the 60s and 70s going undercover in ways similar to the elaborate methods of Detectives Starsky and Hutchinson. The true-life detectives would write a book about their career in *Cop Team* (1975, Pinnacle). Armed with an attorney, the pair approached the producers of the show and were eventually awarded $10,000 each.

The show became known for not only its charismatic and talented leads, but also the 1975 Ford Gran Torino, referred occasionally in-show as "The Striped Tomato." While I will leave the specifics of the legendary vehicle to better hands, it's worth noting that both stars disliked driving the car, particularly Paul Michael Glaser, who had most of the driving duties. At least 10 Gran Torinos were used during the show's production, and while Starsky's Gran Torino got the lion's share of screen-time, Hutch's late-for-its-own-burial 1973 Ford Galaxie 500 would show up from time to time for comic relief, if nothing else. Merchandise would come in the form of action figures, toy cars, and tie-in novels, which have all become collector's items to some extent.

Like many TV shows in the 70s, many actors who would later become stars themselves would have small parts or guest shots on the show. Everyone from Lynda Carter and Suzanne Somers to Mare Winningham and Jeffrey Tambor all made appearances along with the likes of John Ritter and Kim Cattrall. Some of the notable actors and those on the production/staff writers are mentioned in their respective episodes.

Starsky and Hutch benefitted not only from the dynamic of its leads and regular supporting cast members Antonio Fargas and Bernie Hamilton, and featured classic set pieces such as Hutch's frantic run from pay phone to pay phone in "The Psychic" (2.15); Starsky's speech to his fellow officers as they search for a hitman-who holds the key to a cure to a virus that has Hutch close to death in "The Plague Part One" (3.9); the dynamic between Hutch and a wounded Starsky trying to get the control of an uncontrollable situation in "The Shootout" (1.14) and the *neo-noir* of Starsky confronting Carla in "Survival" (2.16).

While the questions in this book can range from easy to difficult, the author wishes first and foremost the intent to be one of fun, nostalgia, and appreciation. This book excludes the 2004 film. Credits are as per IMDb and episodes listed are in broadcast order. This is notable as there can be differences in sequence in home media sources, including streaming. All questions are in order of occurrence in the respective episode.

This book is not meant as a study of timelines and continuity, as the show was produced in a much different creative environment than the more interactive kind we see in contemporary fandom.

Whether it's in the Gran Torino or the Galaxie 500 with the inconvenient horn malfunction, I hope you enjoy the ride.

CAST

David Soul as Detective Sergeant Ken "Hutch" Hutchinson

Paul Michael Glaser as Detective Sergeant Dave Starsky

Antonio Fargas as Huggy Bear

Richard Ward as Captain Dobey

SEASON ONE

1.0 "Pilot"

Director: Barry Shear

Writer: William Blinn

SELECTED SUPPORTING CAST:

Michael Lerner as Fat Rolly

Gordon Jump as Vinny

Buddy Lester as Coley

Michael Conrad as Cannell

Gilbert Green as Tallman

Richard Lynch as Zane (uncredited)

Morgan Sterne as D.A. Mark Henderson (as Albert Morgenstern)

Richard Lynch would also appear in episodes "Quadromania" (3.21) and Starsky vs. Hutch." (4.21.)

Gilbert Green is also in "Snowstorm" (1.4.).

Michael Lerner as Fat Rolly would return in "Texas Longhorn" (1.2.).

Gordon Jump would go on to star in *WKRP in Cincinnati*.

SYNOPSIS

When hitmen kill a couple in a car identical to the striped Gran Torino they drive, detectives Dave Starsky and Ken Hutchinson realize it was they who were the targets and that the assassins are still at large.

1 Q: Which movie are the two gunmen discussing in the first scene?

2 Q: To which gym does Starsky go to find Hutch?

3 Q: What does Starsky offer Hutch during Hutch's workout?

4 Q: Whose car do they take after the gym?

5 Q: What items do they inventory in the car?

6 Q: What is their call sign?

7 Q: At what time does Starsky report to the station that he and Hutch are on patrol?

8 Q: What are the names of the two women Starsky and Hutch mention at the start of their patrol?

9 Q: What is the name of the first suspect they talk to?

10 Q: What is the license plate on Hutch's car?

11 Q: Into what kind of establishment do they follow Rolly?

12 Q: How does Hutch know Rolly wrote a particular note?

13 Q: Over what kind of table does Starsky question Rolly?

14 Q: Which basketball game does Rolly say he bet on?

15 Q: How many Scotches does Hutch say Rolly's had?

16 Q: What is the license plate on the victim's Gran Torino?

17 Q: What color is the phone on Hutch's desk?

18 Q: Hutch refers to his ex-wife by what name?

19 Q: In what kind of room does Tallman meet Starsky and Hutch?

20 Q: At which age does Tallman say his father died?

21 Q: What is the weather during the narco stakeout?

22 Q: What is the name of the dog being walked during the stakeout?

23 Q: Who is positioned behind the dog's favorite tree?

24 Q: Who takes the masked man into the pool?

25 Q: What code word does Starsky shout to tell Hutch to take cover?

26 Q: Where do they meet with Huggy Bear?

27 Q: In the theatre, from what is the woman behind Starsky and Hutch drinking?

28 Q: What football position does Starsky say he played in high school?

29 Q: Which route does Hutch take outside the hotel?

30 Q: What color jacket does Hutch wear during the pursuit?

31 Q: On which floor does Henderson exit the elevator?

32 Q: On what does Hutch land when he jumps from the fire escape?

33 Q: What is Frankie doing when Starsky and Hutch return to the gym?

34 Q: What's the last thing Hutch says to Starsky?

1.1 "Savage Sunday"

(Regular cast now features Bernie Hamilton as Capt. Harold Dobey)

Director: Jack Starrett (as Claude Ennis Starrett Jr.)

Writer: Fred Freiberger

SELECTED SUPPORTING CAST:

Arthur Peterson as Henny Wilson

Hope Summers as Sarah Wilson

Ray Vitte as Tony

T.J. Castronovo as Marty (as Tom Castronova)

Dick Wesson as Ed

Suzanne Somers as Sally Ann Sloane

Louis James Oliver as Ted

Edward Walsh as Wilbur Sloane

Bob Delegall as Gregg Morton

Erik Kilpatrick as Huey (as Eric Kilpatrick)

Eddie Lo Russo as Milty (Uncredited)

Suzanne Somers also starred in the episodes "The Vampire" (2.7) and "Murder Ward" (3.4) and would go on to star in *Three's Company.*

SYNOPSIS

Starsky and Hutch must find a stolen car which, unbeknownst to the thieves, has a trunkful of dynamite set to detonate in a few hours.

1 Q: Which section of the newspaper is Hutch reading in the opening scene?

2 Q: What kind of tie does Henny wear?

3 Q: How many sticks of dynamite are in the trunk of Sarah and Henny's car?

4 Q: What color is Sarah's hat?

5 Q: Who chases Milty down the alley?

6 Q: How much money does Ted say he makes an hour?

7 Q: In what color do Wilbur and Greg have the car repainted?

8 Q: What does Hutch ask Starsky for while taking a witness statement at the liquor store?

9 Q: What year is Henny and Sarah's car?

10 Q: Who does Hutch call when he hears about the dynamite in the car?

11 Q: At what time will the dynamite go off?

12 Q: What does Huggy Bear tell Starsky and Hutch happens when they walk into his bar?

13 Q: What kind of fast food do Starsky and Hutch get?

14 Q: What does Hutch do with Starsky's food?

15 Q: How much is the bet they make with Huey and Tony on the basketball court?

16 Q: At which place is the bookie joint?

17 Q: What is Starsky eating at The Princess Discotheque?

18 Q: What does Hutch throw at Starsky in the alley?

19 Q: Which state's plates does Ted tell Starsky and Hutch he put on the repainted car?

20 Q: According to Dobey, how many men are on alert?

21 Q: What does Starsky steal from Dobey?

22 Q: What is the Police Emergency phone number?

23 Q: What kind of vehicle is the police officer escorting Starsky and Hutch to the parking garage driving?

24 Q: Who drives Henny and Sarah's car out of the parking garage?

25 Q: What does Hutch yell at the motorcycle escort?

26 Q: What does Starsky crash the car through?

27 Q: Which team does Hutch tell Wilber won the basketball game?

28 Q: In the last scene, or tag, who is in attendance as a food expert during the councilman's lunch at Eastside Home for the Aged?

1.2 "Texas Longhorn"

Director: Jack Starrett (as Claude Ennis Starrett Jr.)

Writer: Michael Mann

Writer Michael Mann would go on to pen the episodes "Lady Blue" (1.10), Jojo" (1.19), and "The Psychic" (2.15), before earning acclaim with films like *Thief* (1981), *Manhunter* (1986), *Heat* (1995), and *Collateral* (2004). He was also executive producer and writer on TV's *Miami Vice* (1984-89.).

SELECTED SUPPORTING CAST

Med Flory as Zack Tyler

George Loros as Little Huey Chaco

Charles Napier as John Brown Harris

Michael Lerner as Fat Rolly

Ann Weldon as Angel

Nora Denney as Ray aka Tattoo Woman (as Dodo Denney)

Bobby Hall as Marty

George Loros would also act in the episode "The Psychic" (2.15).

SYNOPSIS

A pair of rapist/murderers are hunted by not only Starsky and Hutch, but the vengeance-fueled husband of their victim.

1 Q: To what fairy tale item does Starsky compare the boot toe piece?

2 Q: Who throws Marty through the office door?

3 Q: What does Starsky "borrow" from Fat Rolly?

4 Q: By what article of clothing does Hutch grab Fat Rolly?

5 Q: How much does Ray charge the customer getting a tattoo?

6 Q: What does Ray keep in her mouth throughout the tattoo studio scene?

7 Q: What does Starsky do to the uncooperative phone booth?

8 Q: Which pro football player does Huggy tell them he's meaner than?

9 Q: What color are Starsky's shoes?

10 Q: What does Capt. Dobey say Starsky's report reads like?

11 Q: In which hand does Starsky carry his gun?

12 Q: What does Starsky slide across the countertop to Chaco?

13 Q: What does Starsky hit Chaco with during questioning?

14 Q: By what number does Hutch refer to Chaco?

15 Q: For what does Fat Rolly say Harris sells his blood?

16 Q: what type of machine does Starsky punch repeatedly?

17 Q: Whose gun does Hutch end up using when his own is empty?

18 Q: The story Zack tells involves which two animals?

19 Q: In the tag, who is shooting pool when Starsky and Hutch enter Huggy's bar?

1.3 "Death Ride"

Director: Gene Nelson

Writer: Edward J. Lasco

SELECTED SUPPORTING CAST

Kathleen Mello as Joanne Mello/Linda Williams

Paul Hecht as D.A. Coleman

Joseph Bova as George (as Joe Bova)

E.J. André as Jenson (as E.J. Endre)

Mary Margaret Lewis as Terry Evers

Charlie Picerni as Thug #1 (uncredited)

Charlie Picerni was Paul Michael Glaser's stunt double and would appear in 92 episodes in various capacities on the show, including director of "Partners" (3.20) and "Birds of a Feather" (4.15).

SYNOPSIS

Starsky and Hutch are assigned to escort the daughter of a crime boss from San Francisco to LA.

1 Q: How much did Starsky's watch cost?

2 Q: What color is Andrew Mello's limousine?

3 Q: To which hospital is Mello taken?

4 Q: What is the name of the TV show on which Huggy plans to appear?

5 Q: Under which arm does Hutch carry his gun?

6 Q: What is Starsky's response when Hutch tells him to relax?

7 Q: Who does Starsky say he and Hutch can trust?

8 Q: Who carries Joanne Mello's suitcase?

9 Q: How many cars pursue the taxi?

10 Q: What is the cab driver's name?

11 Q: What word does Hutch yell to alert Starsky to the gunmen in the Chevy?

12 Q: What item of Starsky's does Hutch give to George?

13 Q: Who carries Joanne's purse out of the diner?

14 Q: What does Starsky use to simulate the sounds of working on a car?

15 Q: What kind of footwear is Starsky wearing?

16 Q: What drink does Joanne say she wants?

17 Q: Which TV doctor does Starsky reference in the hospital?

18 Q: What does Joanne/Linda Williams say when Hutch asks if her gunshot wound hurts.

19 Q: In the tag, which video game are Starsky and Hutch playing at Huggy's?

1.4 "Snowstorm"

Director: Bob Kelljan

Writer: Robert I. Holt

SELECTED SUPPORTING CAST

George Dzunda as Crandell

Paul Benjamin as Detective Burke

Gilbert Green as Stryker

Jim Bohan as Freddie

Bill Sorrells as Detective Kalowitz

Richard Venture as Detective Corman

SYNOPSIS

After a million dollars in cocaine goes missing, Starsky and Hutch have 48 hours to solve the case.

1 Q: How many total plainclothes detectives are at the stakeout?

2 Q: What breed of dog does Hutch see repeatedly?

3 Q: Why does Starsky not want to be the bad cop while questioning Crandall?

4 Q: How many cars block Starsky and Hutch in the parking garage?

5 Q: How much is Stryker's last offer to them to "return" his merchandise?

6 Q: How much value does Stryker say the coke has?

7 Q: Who tells Starsky and Hutch about "the meat plant"?

8 Q: Where in the abandoned shack does Crandell hide the missing drugs?

9 Q: What kind of business does Starsky say his uncle has?

10 Q: What does Hutch call Starsky's car while they wait for Crandall?

11 Q: How do Starsky and Hutch enter the shack?

12 Q: Where does Burke tell Corman to ditch the gun?

13 Q: Who calls the station after they save Huggy?

14 Q: Who puts the cuffs on Stryker?

15 Q: What was Dobey's late partner's name?

16 Q: How many shots does Starsky fire at Burke?

17 Q: In the tag, who's eating with Starsky and Hutch at Huggy's?

18 Q: How many times total does Hutch see the Dalmatian?

1.5 "The Fix"

Director: William Craig

Writer: Robert I. Holt

SELECTED SUPPORTING CAST

Robert Loggia as Ben Forest

Geoffrey Lewis as Monk

Leigh Christian as Jeanie Walton

Gino Conforti as Mickey (as Gene Conforti)

Anthony Charnota as Coney

Film and TV actor Robert Loggia would also be seen in "The Groupie" (4.10).

While possibly inspired by *The French Connection II* (opening 5/21/75 against this episode's original airdate of 10/8/75) this is an episode notable for the performances of its two leads, and particularly David Soul.

SYNOPSIS

A ruthless drug kingpin has Hutch kidnapped and forcibly addicted to heroin.

1 Q: For how much money does Starsky ask from Hutch in the opening scene?

2 Q: What does Starsky do to get the vending machine to give him a candy bar?

3 Q: What does Starsky say will put Hutch "in the poorhouse"?

4 Q: After being kidnapped, who does Hutch insist he is during questioning?

5 Q: What game is Huggy playing when Starsky goes to talk to him?

6 Q: What does Starsky find in Hutch's house that convinces him something's wrong?

7 Q: At what location does Hutch say Jeanie can be found?

8 Q: How much does Starsky offer Mickey for information?

9 Q: Where does Starsky take Hutch to recuperate?

10 Q: What does Hutch knock out of Starsky's hand?

11 Q: What game is Starsky trying to occupy the time with a withdrawing Hutch?

12 Q: What does Starsky ask Huggy to bring more of?

13 Q: Which shoe is Starsky missing when he calls Dobey?

14 Q: What does Hutch insist Huggy Bear call for him?

15 Q: In the tag, what is the last thing Starsky asks Hutch?

1.6 "Death Notice"

Director: William Crain

Writer: Robert C. Dennis

SELECTED SUPPORTING CAST

Ivor Francis as Anton Rusz

Milt Kogan as Manny

Lenore Kasdorf as Kathi

Suzanne Charny as Ginger

Vincent Baggetta as Jerry Neilan

Roz Kelly as Francine

Walter Brooke as David Delano

Suzanne Charny would appear in "The Game" (4.2).

Roz Kelly appeared in episodes "The Las Vegas Strangler Parts 1 and 2" (2.1, 2.2) and "Fatal Charm" (3.2).

SYNOPSIS

Starsky and Hutch investigate the murders of strippers and the man who issues warnings about them.

1 Q: What is the name of the first dancer we see?

2 Q: What message does Anton leave?

3 Q: What sort of accent does Ginger have?

4 Q: What is Francine wearing around her neck when Starsky and Hutch talk to her in the dressing room?

5 Q: On which cheek does Anton have a scar?

6 Q: Who breaks the news of Ginger's death to the club staff?

7 Q: Who notices someone from the staff is missing?

8 Q: At Delano's meat plant, who throws one of the thugs into a Dumpster?

9 Q: By what famous comedian's first name does Hutch refer to Starsky at Superior Meats?

10 Q: Who is the first to climb the ladder outside the club?

11 Q: When are the times Hutch says he's afraid of heights?

12 Q: Who flips a coin to see who goes first through the roof access?

13 Q: What is Hutch holding in his teeth when they question Anton?

14 Q: From where is Anton hearing the voices?

15 Q: What was Anton doing with the mannequins?

16 Q: Whose name does Starsky get wrong consistently?

17 Q: What is Starsky drinking when Hutch offers him coffee?

18 Q: What sort of sign does Starsky say Kathi metaphorically pointed at Ginger?

19 Q: To what does Hutch cuff Delano?

20 Q: What piece of landscaping does Posey try to climb when Starsky and Hutch get the drop on him?

21 Q: In the tag, which song are Starsky and Hutch singing?

22 Q: Who is wearing Francine's headphones?

23 Q: What does Anton say are the ingredients for his goulash?

1.7 "Pariah"

Director: Bob Kelljan

Writer: Michael Fisher

SELECTED SUPPORTING CAST

Stephen McNally as George Prudholm

Gregory Rozakis as Joseph Tramaine

Hilda Haynes as Eunice Craig

Graham Jarvis as City Attorney Collins

John Alderman as Cecil

Jay Fletcher as Tidings

Antra Ford as Molly

Stephen McNally would return as George Prudholm in "Starsky's Lady" (2.19).

SYNOPSIS

A man from Starsky's past takes advantage for revenge after the uproar caused by Starsky killing a young Black thief.

1 Q: What is Starsky holding in his mouth while going through his fridge?

2 Q: In which appliance does Hutch fix his breakfast?

3 Q: Who has the shotgun when Starsky and Hutch arrive at the liquor store?

4 Q: Who attends to the fallen uniformed officer?

5 Q: In court, what does Hutch wave to Starsky?

6 Q: How many times does the judge bang the gavel before the verdict is read?

7 Q: What one word does Starsky whisper to Dobey as he leaves his office?

8 Q: What two words does Cecil use to greet them?

9 Q: Who covers the front when Tremaine flees?

10 Q: How many uniformed police meet Starsky and Hutch at the market?

11 Q: Who attacks Tremaine during questioning?

12 Q: What is Prudholm's room number?

13 Q: Who finds the ammunition in Prudholm's room?

14 Q: Where does Prudholm say he'll meet Starsky?

15 Q: Who steals a police car to trail Starsky?

16 Q: In the tag, which drink does Hutch make for Starsky?

1.8 "Kill Huggy Bear"

Director: Michael Schultz

Writer: Fred Freiberger

SELECTED SUPPORTING CAST

Dick Anthony Williams as Harry Martin

Gloria Edwards as Sarah Kingston

Hamilton Camp as Lou Malinda

Roger Robinson as Dewey Hughes

SYNOPSIS

Set-up for a crime he didn't commit, Huggy Bear turns to Starsky and Hutch for help.

1 Q: Which two units' call signs are dispatched to the robbery?

2 Q: Who drives the Gran Torino to the crime scene?

3 Q: Which snack is on the bar when Dewey talks to Huggy?

4 Q: Whose car does Dewey steal?

5 Q: What kind of red does Starsky say his car is painted in?

6 Q: What is Huggy doing when Starsky and Hutch come into his bar?

7 Q: What does Starsky do to keep Huggy from continuing his game?

8 Q: Where do they take Huggy to keep him safe?

9 Q: What does Malinda's man give to them to drink?

10 Q: What does Malinda say Huggy's run out of?

11 Q: To whom does Starsky give his carrot juice?

12 Q: What two supplements does Hutch tell Starsky he takes?

13 Q: What does Hutch tell Starsky to do with "machismo"?

14 Q: What do Starsky and Hutch argue about after they realize the brakes are out?

15 Q: In the tag, to what does Hutch help himself when he and Starsky take Huggy to see Malinda?

1.9 "The Bait"

Director: Ivan Dixon

Writers: (Teleplay) James Schmerer & Don Balluck and Edward J. Lasko

(Story) James Schmerer & Don Balluck

Director Ivan Dixon's name may be more familiar to audiences as Sgt. James Kinchloe on TV's *Hogan's Heroes* from 1965 to 1970.

SELECTED SUPPORTING CAST

Lynne Marta as Cheryl Waite

Charles Macaulay as Danner (as Charles McCaulay)

Akili Jones as Connie

Michael DeLano as Billy Harkness

David S. Cass Sr. as Shockley (as Dave Cass)

Lynne Marta would appear in "Murder at Sea, Parts 1 and 2" (2.3, 2.4) and "Quadromania" (3.21) and was David Soul's girlfriend at the time.

SYNOPSIS

Starsky and Hutch go undercover to get to the head of a heroin syndicate.

1 Q: In which part of his foot does Starsky say his shoes are hurting him?

2 Q: How many police officers arrest them?

3 Q: What does Starsky tell a cop at the station to not forget to book?

4 Q: To whose coffee does Starsky help himself in Dobey's office?

5 Q: What is the name and year of the stamp being sought?

6 Q: What does Capt. Dobey order at Huggy's?

7 Q: A poster of what legendary guitarist is in the stairwell of Huggy's bar?

8 Q: What does Starsky look for in Cheryl's kitchen?

9 Q: For how long does Cheryl say it's been since she's seen Joanne?

10 Q: How does Starsky wake up Billy?

11 Q: At what time does Billy tell them to meet him at the warehouse?

12 Q: Who fires the first shot at the warehouse?

13 Q: What do Starsky and Hutch use as a moving obstacle at the warehouse?

14 Q: Who hands Danner the museum's stamp?

15 Q: What color is Cheryl's suitcase?

16 Q: In the tag, what does Hutch say one of Starsky's friends called their combination of Irish coffee and chicken soup?

1.10 "Lady Blue"

Director: Don Weis

Writer: Michael Mann

SELECTED SUPPORTING CAST

James Keach as James March Wrightwood

Quinn K. Redeker as Dr. Melford (as Quinn Redeker)

Timothy Blake as Cindy

Elisha Cook Jr. as Polly the Snitch (as Elisha Cook)

Tony Ballen as Wally

Ed Bakey as Fifth Avenue

Richard Karron as John Slow

Quinn K. Redeker would also appear in "Targets Without a Badge, Part 1" (4.18).

Richard Karron would be seen again in "The Golden Angel" (4.13).

SYNOPSIS

An ex-girlfriend of Starsky's is found murdered and bound with television antenna wire and it's up to Starsky and Hutch to find the killer.

1 Q: In the opening scene, for how long does Hutch say he's been on hold?

2 Q: What is the name of Huggy Bear's friend who he says can fix Hutch's car?

3 Q: What call sign does Starsky speculate they could have been assigned?

4 Q: What is the name of the club Helen worked?

5 Q: What does Cindy show Starsky that upsets him?

6 Q: What does Polly say Commander Jim is "into"?

7 Q: What does Polly yell for Hutch to put down?

8 Q: What does Jim have wrapped around his legs when they go to see him?

9 Q: What does Huggy serve Starsky at The Pits?

10 Q: Who drives the car off Wally's lot?

11 Q: What item of Hutch's does Fifth Avenue steal, then makes a point of returning to Hutch?

12 Q: What is House Three's appraisal of Starsky's command of Spanish?

13 Q: What unusual thing does Hutch notice about the radio in Helen's car?

14 Q: With what does Hutch break a window into Jim's?

15 Q: What color does Jim say his eyes bleed?

16 Q: From where does Jim say the waves are coming?

17 Q: On the radio tower, who keeps Jim talking while the hostage is rescued?

18 Q: In the tag, how did Hutch find out Starsky's favorite dish?

19 Q: What piece of motherly advice does Hutch give to Starsky just before the freeze-frame?

1.11 "Captain Dobey, You're Dead!"

Director: Michael Schultz

Writer: Michael Fisher

SELECTED SUPPORTING CAST

William Watson as Leo Moon

Lynn Hamilton as Edith Dobey

William Traylor as Norris (as Bill Traylor)

Kurt Grayson as Marty Pommier

Lester Rollins as C.J. Woodfield

Taaffe O'Connell as Lola Brenner

Claire Touchstone as Rosie Dobey

Eric Suter as Cal Dobey (as Eric Sutter)

SYNOPSIS

Starsky and Hutch must find a former cop escaped from prison before he can wreak vengeance upon Captain Dobey and his family.

1 Q: Which book does Hutch toss to Starsky?

2 Q: Where does Dobey go after his meeting with Miss Sutton?

3 Q: Who takes the candy he buys?

4 Q: Who helps Dobey with his tie?

5 Q: Who does Edith say is the boss of the house?

6 Q: What does Dobey have to step over as he leaves the house?

7 Q: Who moves the bikes?

8 Q: On what TV show does Hutch tell Starsky he was on?

9 Q: What game is being played at the massage parlor?

10 Q: Who fires the gun at Moon after he breaks the Dobeys' window?

11 Q: When Moon calls the Dobey house, who hands Dobey the receiver?

12 Q: What item is Hutch holding when Rosie comes downstairs?

13 Q: For what does Hutch ask at Woodfield's table?

14 Q: Where does Woodfield keep his gun?

15 Q: Who reads Woodfield his rights?

16 Q: In the tag, what game is the Dobey family playing?

17 Q: Whose birthday is it?

18 Q: What does Starsky wag at Capt. Dobey in greeting?

19 Q: Which of the Dobey family is revealed to be left-handed?

1.12 "Terror on the Docks"

Director: Randal Kleiser

Writer: Fred Freiberger

SELECTED SUPPORTING CAST

Stephen McHattie as William 'Billy' Michael Desmond

Sheila Larken as Nancy Blake

Sarah Cunningham as Maureen Blake

Henry Olek as Rick Hauser

Garry Walberg as Earl Banks

Kenneth Tobey as Andy Wilkins

SYNOPSIS

A longtime friend of Hutch's is marrying someone that could be involved in several robberies and the homicide of a police officer.

1 Q: In the first scene, where in the church is Hutch sitting?

2 Q: Who stands in for Nancy's fiancé Billy at the rehearsal?

3 Q: What is the name of the organ player?

4 Q: Who walks Nancy down the aisle?

5 Q: What famous horror actor does Hutch suggest decorated Ezra's pad?

6 Q: What happens when Starsky and Hutch get to the front door of Ezra's church?

7 Q: What happens when Starsky lifts the skull from the altar?

8 Q: What tips Starsky to Billy being a suspect?

9 Q: What effect does Hutch tell Billy he has on him?

10 Q: What is Nancy's reaction to Hutch telling her he doesn't think Billy will show up to the wedding?

11 Q: What does Capt. Dobey suggest an ailing Starsky drink?

12 Q: Who does Skylar tell Starsky and Hutch he was a fool to trust?

13 Q: Who chases Billy in the Gran Torino?

14 Q: In the tag, how does Maureen Blake refer to Starsky?

15 Q: Who gets hit in the face with the cake at the freeze-frame?

1.13 "The Deadly Imposter"

Director: Dick Moder

Writers: (Teleplay) Michael Fisher & Parke Perine and Mann Rubin (Story) Mann Rubin

SELECTED SUPPORTING CAST

Art Hindle as John Colby

Susan Gailey as Karen Karpel (as Suzan Gaily)

Peter Brandon as Warren G. Karpel

Jana Bellan as Jackie

Raymond Singer as Emile Parouch

Ned Wertimer as Buckland

SYNOPSIS

A friend from their Academy days asks Starsky and Hutch for help in finding his ex-wife.

1 Q: In the opening scene, by what name does Mrs. McMillon refer to Starsky?

2 Q: Where in Vinnie's Gym is John Colby when Starsky and Hutch go to see him?

3 Q: For how long was John in a POW camp?

4 Q: What were John, Starsky, and Hutch called in the Academy?

5 Q: What does John have concealed in a newspaper before the attack on the man in the phone booth?

6 Q: To which animal does Jackie compare John?

7 Q: When John acts drunk to Huggy Bear, how does he refer to Starsky and Hutch?

8 Q: What message does Starsky say he knocks on Parouch's door in Morse code?

9 Q: What desk decoration of Garvin's does John examine?

10 Q: Where does Parouch say Karpel is located?

11 Q: What is the license plate on the Gran Torino?

12 Q: Which people are the ones John says he doesn't kill?

13 Q: What does Starsky take from Hutch when they arrest John?

14 Q: In the tag, what does Hutch tell Mrs. McMillon's friend's name is?

1.14 "The Shootout"

Director: Fernando Lamas

Writer: David P. Harmon

Fernando Lamas was known for his romantic roles as an actor in films such as *The Story of the Tango* (1949) and *The Merry Widow* (1952.)

SELECTED SUPPORTING CAST

Albert Paulsen as Tom Lockly

Jess Walton as Theresa Defusto

Steven Keats as Joey Martin

Norman Fell as Sammy Grovner

Barbara Rhoades as Robin Morton

Steve Sandor as Jimmy Lee Carson

Tresa Hughes as Mrs. Durant

Danny Wells as Jeru Maharaji/Harry Sample

Actor Norman Fell may be most familiar to some as Mr. Roper on *Three's Company.*

One of the best episodes of the series and a fan favorite in the *Starsky and Hutch* canon.

SYNOPSIS

Hutch and a wounded Starsky are among those held hostage in a restaurant soon to be the scene of an ambush of a mob boss by two hitmen.

1 Q: Who plays the "Bad Cop" when Starsky and Hutch question Harry?

2 Q: What does Starsky pick up and throw to the floor before leaving Harry's interrogation?

3 Q: How does Starsky pronounce "Lugosi"?

4 Q: When Joey listens to the radio, which teams are playing?

5 Q: At what time is Mr. Monte due to arrive at the restaurant?

6 Q: What is Jimmy drinking?

7 Q: Who IDs Starsky and Hutch as cops?

8 Q: Which wine does Hutch order?

9 Q: How many times does Joey fire at Starsky?

10 Q: What does Hutch put under Starsky's head as a pillow?

11 Q: To whom does Starsky compare with Hutch when he yells?

12 Q: Who killed Theresa's brother?

13 Q: With whom does Joey sit over some wine?

14 Q: What does Hutch give to Starsky before he hands him the water pitcher?

15 Q: Where does Starsky say Gene Autry always got shot?

16 Q: For how long does Theresa say "the Old Man's gun" has gone unused?

17 Q: What does Sammy say his mother used to give him whenever he was sick or injured?

18 Q: What does Sammy say in response to Robin's request to tell her something that will make her laugh?

19 Q: What character does Starsky say he once portrayed in school?

20 Q: What does Theresa do to provide a distraction?

21 Q: In the tag, what does Huggy reveal to be Starsky's middle name?

22 Q: Of what school does Huggy say Starsky is a recent graduate?

23 Q: Which of Starsky's arms is in a sling?

1.15 "The Hostages"

Director: George McCowan

Writer: Edward J. Lakso

SELECTED SUPPORTING CAST

John Ritter as Tom Cole

Linda Kelsey as Ellie Cole

Will Hare as Ames

Nellie Bellflower as Sweet Alice

Susan Peretz as Madame Yarm/Mary Polanski

Kristy McNichol as Meg

Melissa Newman as Amy

John Ritter would go on to star in films and TV, notably in *Three's Company* and *8 Simple Rules*.

Nellie Bellflower would portray the character of Sweet Alice again in "A Coffin for Starsky" (1.21).

This is Kristy McNichol's first of three appearances on the show. She would also appear in "Little Girl Lost" (2.13) and "The Trap" (3.15) and went on to star on TV's *Family*.

SYNOPSIS

Starsky and Hutch must find a way to help an armored car driver blackmailed by the men who have kidnapped his wife.

1 Q: According to the DJ on the radio in the opening scene, what time is it?

2 Q: For what armored car service does Tom work ?

3 Q: Who calls Dobey after they find Harry's body?

4 Q: In which city does Hutch say the Abbott armored car robbery took place?

5 Q: How often does Tom say the man who is driving with him makes phone calls?

6 Q: After Tom meets Starsky and Hutch, which of them help load the armored car?

7 Q: When going to Tom's house, what does Starsky say his cover will be?

8 Q: What does Hutch tell him to use as a cover instead?

9 Q: What is Meg repairing when Starsky and Hutch speak to her?

10 Q: Who tells Mr. Ames they don't care what happens to his money when lives are on the line?

11 Q: What does Sweet Alice call Hutch?

12 Q: What type of work does Sweet Alice say she's doing?

13 Q: How did Mary come up with the alias for her fortune-teller scam?

14 Q: What three words does Starsky say to Belle?

15 Q: Who shoots out the armored car's tire?

16 Q: In the tag, how much weight does Dobey say he lost the week before?

17 Q: What number is on Dobey's office door?

18 Q: Who is first out of the doorway to catch Capt. Dobey buying candy?

19 Q: For how much was the bet between Starsky and Hutch?

1.16 "Losing Streak"

Director: Don Weis

Writers: (Teleplay) Michael Fisher

(Story) Robert I. Holt (as Robert I. Holt)

SELECTED SUPPORTING CAST

Dane Clark as Vic Rankin

Arthur Roberts as Mr. White (as Arthur David Roberts)

Zitto Kazann as Gordon Foote

Jacqueline Scott as Evelyn Rankin

Madlyn Rhue as Belinda Williams

Connie Hoffman as Orange (as Connie Lisa Marie)

Roberto Rodriguez as Club Patron (uncredited)

Connie Hoffman would reprise her role as Orange in "Running" (1.20).

Roberto Rodriguez was also seen in "The Velvet Jungle" (2.22), "The Collector" (3.10), and "Class in Crime" (3.17).

SYNOPSIS

An idol from Starsky's childhood becomes a target when he steals counterfeit money from the mob.

1 Q: Who is the first character to speak in this episode?

2 Q: What are Starsky and Hutch eating in the car?

3 Q: What does Toby say he'll play a few yards of after Vic leaves?

4 Q: On which letter of the license plate of the car belonging to White's thugs do Starsky and Hutch disagree?

5 Q: What is the title of Vic's LP Hutch is holding?

6 Q: What color is Evelyn Rankin's robe?

7 Q: Olivia says Starsky is as cute as a what?

8 Q: For how long does Evelyn say she's been with Vic?

9 Q: At what jazz club does Huggy meet Starsky and Hutch?

10 Q: What companion does Orange have?

11 Q: By what sarcastic nickname does Starsky identify Belinda to Hutch?

12 Q: What does Starsky tell White what happens when White lies?

13 Q: What is Hutch's response to Starsky telling him, "Stranger things have happened."

14 Q: What is Huggy doing when Starsky and Hutch meet with him again?

15 Q: Where does Hutch find Vic's blood?

16 Q: What is Vic hiding behind when White brings Belinda to the Mardi Gras Ballroom?

17 Q: In the tag, who is sitting across from Evelyn at Vic's?

1.17 "Silence"

Director: George McCowan

Writers: (Teleplay) Parke Perine

(Story) Donald R. Boyle

SELECTED SUPPORTING CAST

Carl Betz as Father Ignatius

Jason Bernard as R.C. Turner

Chuck McCann as Larry Horvath

Jack DeLeon as Herman Bessinger

Ann Foster as Abigail Crabtree

Doodles Weaver as Eddie Hoyle

Chuck McCann would appear in "Murder on Stage 17" (2.24).

Ann Foster would further portray Abigail Crabtree in "The Deadly Imposter" 1.13, "Bounty Hunter" (1.22), and "Vendetta" (2.10).

Doodles Weaver as Eddie Hoyle would return in "Gillian" (2.5).

SYNOPSIS

A fake priest sets up a deaf man in his care for his own crimes.

1 Q: Who writes the report on Larry Horvath?

2 Q: Who does Hutch tell to stay out of the questioning?

3 Q: What does Larry give to Hutch before leaving with Father Ignatius and R.C.?

4 Q: What does Starsky tear during the foot chase in the alley?

5 Q: On which part of the Gran Torino does Hutch walk, much to the irritation of Starsky?

6 Q: What is in the box that Larry is guarding?

7 Q: Which Bible verse does Jessie recite?

8 Q: For what does Capt. Dobey tell Hutch he doesn't have time?

9 Q: Who catches Dobey eating Starsky's sandwich?

10 Q: For how long does Starsky tell Hutch they've been playing shuffleboard at the Glitter Club?

11 Q: As what famous crime-solving duo does Ignatius refer to Starsky and Hutch sarcastically?

12 Q: In what sort of business do Starsky, Hutch, and R.C. look for Larry?

13 Q: How old would the real Fr. Ignatius be?

14 Q: What is the imposter's real first name?

15 Q: At the movie theatre, what does Starsky throw at Marty?

16 Q: In the tag, what do Larry and R.C. name after Starsky and Hutch?

17 Q: What happens when Hutch holds one of the kittens?

1.18 "Omaha Tiger"

Director: Don Weis

Writer: Edward J. Lakso

SELECTED SUPPORTING CAST

Dennis Burkley as Eddie Bell

Barbara Babcock as Ellen Forbes

Wynn Irwin as Al Taft

Mary Jo Catlett as Terrible Tessie

James Luisi as Carl Boyce

Thayer David as George Felton

Richard Kiel as Iggy

Sonny Klein as Fireball Cannon

Mary Jo Catlett would also appear in "Starsky and Hutch Are Guilty" (2.15).

Richard Kiel would come to find a famous role as the villain Jaws in the James Bond franchise.

Sonny Klein would return as Fireball in "The Psychic" (2.15).

SYNOPSIS

Starsky and Hutch investigate a string of suspicious deaths in the world of wrestling.

1 Q: By what name does Hutch refer to the fleeing suspect in the opening scene?

2 Q: In which venue is the wrestling match?

3 Q: Which wrestling move does Starsky insist is art?

4 Q: For how many years did Hutch wrestle in college?

5 Q: What is Hutch's response when Starsky asks if he's chicken to go back in the ring with him?

6 Q: Which two holds does Tessie demonstrate on Starsky?

7 Q: How does Tessie know they're cops?

8 Q: What does Hutch trip over as he gets into the ring?

9 Q: What is the name of the business in which they meet with Huggy?

10 Q: What is the name of Huggy Bear's racetrack?

11 Q: What does Hutch do when they realize mistakenly that they're trapped in an airtight room?

12 Q: How much does Starsky say he weighs?

13 Q: What color are Starsky's socks?

14 Q: Who disarms Boyce?

15 Q: In the tag, what does Iggy do when he picks up Starsky?

1.19 "JoJo"

Director: George McCowan

Writer: Michael Mann

SELECTED SUPPORTING CAST

Stephen Davies as JoJo Forentic

Linda Scruggs as Linda Mascelli (as Linda Scruggs-Bogart)

Robert Riesel as Nick Dombarris

Fran Ryan as Stella

Alan Fudge as Bettin

Terry Lumly as Molly

Sherry Bain as Elaine Stroud

Raymond Allen as Merl the Earl

Raymond Allen would appear as Merl the Earl in "Bloodbath" (2.14) and "The Game" (4.2).

We would see Fran Ryan again in "Murder Ward" (3.4) and "Photo Finish" (4.4).

SYNOPSIS

Starsky and Hutch must put a psychopathic rapist away for good.

1 Q: For how long does Starsky say they've been at the stakeout?

2 Q: How does Hutch refer to the federal agents working under Bettin?

3 Q: What is Starsky doing when he and Hutch are getting chewed out by Bettin?

4 Q: What happens to Hutch's car when the driver side door is opened?

5 Q: How does Hutch avoid an attack from Linda?

6 Q: Which martial art does Linda say she's studied?

7 Q: What is Starsky doing when they Spot JoJo on the street?

8 Q: What does Stella the waitress tell Hutch he'll have instead of coffee?

9 Q: What is it specifically about the religious items Huggy Bear is selling that ensures 24-hour protection?

10 Q: What is the name of Starsky's uncle Al's body shop?

11 Q: How does Merl the Earl refer to Starsky's car?

12 Q: What does Starsky grab before knocking on Sulko's door?

13 Q: In the tag, to which classic artist does Starsky compares to Merl's latest paint job?

14 Q: What happens to Hutch's car when he opens the hood?

1.20 "Running"

Director: Don Weis

Writer: Michael Fisher

SELECTED SUPPORTING CAST

Jan Smithers as Sharman Crane

Robert Viharo as Vern DuBois

Lana Wood as Ella

Don Plumley as Texas Kid

Martin Azarow as Packrat

Guillermo San Juan as Kiko Ramos

Connie Hoffman as Orange (as Connie Lisa Marie)

Jan Smithers would become known to viewers later on *WKRP in Cincinnati.*

Guillermo San Juan would return as Kiko Ramos in "Little Girl Lost" (2.13).

SYNOPSIS

Starsky puts his career at risk to help his old friend, Sharman.

1 Q: What does Starsky notice in the water as he and Hutch drive over the bridge?

2 Q: How many kids are sitting with Kiko when Hutch approaches them?

3 Q: What does Starsky offer to buy Hutch for dinner?

4 Q: Whose phone extension is being used in a series of practical jokes?

5 Q: What is the inscription on Sharman's bracelet?

6 Q: What does Orange show them that belongs to Sharman?

7 Q: What is Sharman's room number?

8 Q: How many shots does Vern fire at them through Sharman's door?

9 Q: What does Starsky do with Sharman's bottle of liquor?

10 Q: Which class did Starsky and Sharman share?

11 Q: What is Starsky's address?

12 Q: Who pursues Vern in the Gran Torino when Vern flees?

13 Q: What does Starsky do before Sharman can introduce her parents to him?

14 Q: In the tag, what is Hutch doing while Starsky speaks to his mom on the phone?

15 Q: Who is revealed to be behind the prank with Dobey's extension?

1.21 "A Coffin for Starsky"

Director: George McCowan

Writer: Arthur Rowe

SELECTED SUPPORTING CAST

Jenny Sullivan as Cheryl Jennings

Gene Dynarski as Victor K. Bellamy

Seth Allen as Janos P. Martini

John McLiam as Professor Jennings

Nellie Bellflower as Sweet Alice

SYNOPSIS

After Starsky is injected with a compound that will kill him, he and Hutch have 24 hours to find the criminal responsible and the cure.

1 Q: Who does Starsky call after being injected?

2 Q: Which article of clothing does Starsky ask for back at the hospital?

3 Q: In what kind of business is Huggy employed in this episode?

4 Q: By what name does Dobey call Starsky when they go through the files?

5 Q: Which symptom is Starsky starting to show when they see Bellamy?

6 Q: To whose house do they go after Bellamy's?

7 Q: On the set, what does Janos tell Ginger to get rid of?

8 Q: What item of Janos' do they use to play Keep Away?

9 Q: What color is the stuffed animal Starsky pulls out of his desk?

10 Q: Who kills Bellamy?

11 Q: Who meets Hutch outside the ICU?

12 Q: In the tag, what is Starsky using to appear sicker than he is?

13 Q: What does Hutch pour over Starsky's head?

1.22 "Bounty Hunter"

Director: Don Weis

Writer: Steve Fisher

SELECTED SUPPORTING CAST

Ramon Bieri as Bo Rile

Sherry Jackson as Denise Girard

Lola Albright as Lola Turkel

Stan Ross as Monte Vorhees

Jon Cedar as Jerry Konig

Doodles Weaver as Eddie Hoyle

Jack Kirby as Officer Day

Victoria Wells as Nina (as Victoria Ann Berry)

Ann Foster as Abigail Crabtree

Muffi Durham as Nancy

Beloved character actor Doodles Weaver was also the uncle of actress Sigourney Weaver.

Lola Albright would be familiar to audiences as having played Edie Hart on an earlier TV detective show, *Peter Gunn*.

It may interest some to see legendary comic book artist Jack Kirby have a cameo as Officer Day.

Victoria Wells would later be seen in the episodes "The Las Vegas Strangler Part 1" (2.1) and "The Action" (3.12).

Muffi Durham would be seen again in "The Committee" (2.21).

SYNOPSIS

A bail bonds office is really a front for an extortion racket.

1 Q: The story Starsky reads in the opening scene features an article on what animal being responsible for human deaths more than any other cause?

2 Q: How does Starsky refer to banana chips?

3 Q: What does Hutch say cops are not supposed to be?

4 Q: Who kills Konig?

5 Q: When responding to the silent alarm, who puts the Mars light on top of the car?

6 Q: According to Huggy, what is Bigfoot's true origin and purpose?

7 Q: Which comic book is Monty reading when they visit him in the hotel?

8 Q: What is Hutch eating as he goes through the hotel register?

9 Q: By which names does Eddie refer to Starsky and Hutch?

10 Q: Who pins Bo to Lola's desk?

11 Q: On what corner does Lola tell them the paint factory is located?

12 Q: Who tackles Bo on the stairs?

13 Q: In the tag, which vitamin does Hutch ask Abigail if she added to their drinks?

SEASON TWO

2.1 "The Las Vegas Strangler, Part 1"

Director: George McCowan

Writer: Michael Fisher

SELECTED SUPPORTING CAST

Paul Burke as Lt. Ted Cameron

Frank Converse as Jack Mitchell

Lynda Carter as Vicky

Joan Blondell as Mrs. Pruitt

George Tobias as 'Ace'

Foster Brooks as Drunk Gambler

Darrell as Eugene Pruitt

Roz Kelly as Iris Thayer

Victoria Wells as Sharon Flynn (as Victoria Ann Berry)

Jayne Kennedy as Gretchen Hollander

This episode features a variety of roles filled by beloved performers from both past as well as contemporary film and TV, including Lynda Carter who had made her debut in 1975 as Wonder Woman in TV's *The New Original Wonder Woman.*

SYNOPSIS

The prime suspect in a series of strangulations is an old friend of Hutch's.

1 Q: Which habit of Starsky's has Dobey told him to stop doing?

2 Q: When does Duke say he was last in Las Vegas?

3 Q: Who is driving on their way to Vegas?

4 Q: What game is Starsky playing at the gas station?

5 Q: What fever does Starsky say he has when they're in the casino?

6 Q: Who insists on carrying the money?

7 Q: On what number and color does Starsky bet on at the roulette table?

8 Q: Which game does Hutch play that he seems to have an affinity for?

9 Q: Who starts the fight at the casino?

10 Q: Who's the first to get punched?

11 Q: In high school, what was Hutch voted as?

12 Q: Who notices the two-way mirror in the drunk tank?

13 Q: Dr. Cleveland say Jack's been arrested in Vegas how many times?

14 Q: What physical reaction does Vicky note Starsky as having when they talk to her in the dressing room?

15 Q: In the pool, who does Hutch toss over his shoulder?

16 Q: What is Vicky drinking with her tea when Starsky visits?

17 Q: At what time does Jack say the "real people" come on in Las Vegas?

2.2 "The Las Vegas Strangler, Part 2"

1 Q: Who is trying to sleep in the back of the Edsel?

2 Q: How many times does Vicky say she uses her tea bags?

3 Q: Who arrests "The Strangler" on the casino rooftop?

4 Q: Where is Jack's tumor located?

5 Q: According to the undamaged photo Eugene has, who is to be the next victim?

6 Q: Who feeds Vicky's goldfish during a visit to her apartment?

7 Q: At which casino does Eugene tell Iris he'll meet her?

8 Q: What alerts Starsky and Hutch to Mrs. Pruitt's body?

9 Q: Who asks Eugene if he wants to talk?

10 Q: Who asks sarcastically if he looks like Evel Knievel?

11 Q: Which of the two of them is the first to jump onto the safety net?

12 Q: In the tag, who receives the missing $23,000?

13 Q: At what game do Starsky and Hutch tell Capt. Dobey the money was lost?

2.3 "Murder at Sea, Part 1"

Director: George McCowan

Writer: Ron Friedman

SELECTED SUPPORTING CAST

Jean-Pierre Aumont as Capt. La Rue

Burr DeBenning as Officer Jansen

José Ferrer as Crazy Joey Fortune (as Jose Ferrer)

Will Geer as Commodore Atwater

Lynne Marta as Helen Carnahan

Kay Medord as Edna Zelinka

Ron Moody as Derek Stafford

Robert Walden as Marty Simon

Ed Begley Jr. as Harv Schwab

Paul Picerni as Patsy Cairo

Charlie Picerni as Nicky Cairo (as Charles Picerni)

Ed Begley Jr. would star in *Battlestar Galactica, St. Elsewhere,* and numerous other films and TV.

Paul Picerni was the older brother of Charlie and would also appear in "Starsky and Hutch on Voodoo Island" (3.1).

SYNOPSIS

Starsky and Hutch go undercover as entertainment directors Hack and Zack on a cruise ship to solve a mystery that is more than it seems.

1 Q: What is the name of Percival's cat?

2 Q: Starsky says everybody has a tattoo of what two things?

3 Q: Where does Starsky say Hutch was born?

4 Q: What item distracts Starsky when they visit the commodore?

5 5 Q: What sort of shop has Huggy opened?

6 Q: Who comes up with their cover IDs?

7 Q: To what does Starsky compare their room?

8 Q: What sort of tie does Capt. La Rue wear meeting Starsky and Hutch for the first time?

9 Q: What is the name of the cruise ship?

10 Q: Led by Starsky, what is the first game a group of passengers play?

11 Q: What does Hutch pretend to be doing when caught at Pasty's door?

12 Q: What is Mrs. Clark's performance of in the talent show?

13 Q: What last name does Hutch give for Starsky's Hack?

14 Q: What song is Mr. Takahashi going to sing?

15 Q: When Starsky walks away from the Clarks' door, what tune does he whistle?

16 Q: Who knocks out Starsky?

17 Q: Who finds the unconscious Starsky?

2.4 "Murder at Sea, Part 2"

1 Q: What is Helen doing when Starsky and Hutch go to her room?

2 Q: Who goes through her desk?

3 Q: How many passengers does Crazy Joey bet Nicky will survive?

4 Q: In how many minutes does Joey say the second bomb explodes?

5 Q: What is Hutch's response to Helen when she asks if there's anything she can do?

6 Q: Who finds the third bomb?

7 Q: Who uses a rope to pull the bombs out of the engine room?

8 Q: Who drives the dune buggy when they pursue Fortune and his thugs?

9 Q: In the tag, who is appointed the captain of the Amapola?

10 Q: Who nearly hits Hutch in the face with a sword accidentally?

2.5 "Gillian"

Director: George McCowan

Writers: (Teleplay) Benjamin Messelink (as Ben Masselink)

(Story) Amanda J. Green

SELECTED SUPPORTING CAST

Karen Carlson as Gillian Ingram

Mike Kellin as Al Grossman

Doodles Weaver as Eddie Hoyle

Diana Canova as Nancy Rogers

Joanna Kerns as Joy (as Joanna DeVarona)

Richard Foronjy as Harry Blower

Daina House as Girl (as Dana House)

Marilyn Joi as Pepper

Daina House would also be in "Starsky and Hutch on Voodoo Island" (3.1).

Diana Canova later would star in TV's *Soap*.

Joanna Kearns gained notoriety on the smash TV show, *Growing Pains*.

Karen Carlson was married to David Soul until 1977 and would show up again in "The Heroes" (3.7).

One of the best episodes of the entire canon and shows the range of both lead actors.

SYNOPSIS

Starsky learns a secret about Hutch's new love interest.

1 Q: In the opening scene, which of them is wearing sunglasses?

2 Q: Who gives Nancy bowling lessons?

3 Q: Which part of his car does Hutch walk across after taking Gillian home?

4 Q: What is the name of the shoeshine working on Huggy's shoes?

5 Q: What pendant is on Huggy Bear's necklace?

6 Q: What does Olga offer to Starsky and Hutch?

7 Q: Whom does Starsky call for information on Gillian?

8 Q: How much money does Starsky offer to Gillian?

9 Q: Gillian gives Mrs. Grossman the keys back from which three things?

10 Q: Who does Olga tell to tell Al to kill along with Gillian?

11 Q: What is the name of Hutch's apartment building?

12 Q: Who finds Gillian dead?

13 Q: Who calls Gillian's apartment after she's discovered?

14 Q: What is Gillian's apartment number?

15 Q: Who tells Hutch that Gillian worked for Grossman?

16 Q: What is Hutch's response?

17 Q: In the theatre, what does Starsky use to tie up one of Grossman's thugs?

18 Q: In the tag, what does Nancy call a strike in bowling?

19 Q: What nickname has Nancy given to Starsky?

20 Q: What does Hutch tell the woman in the next lane they call "bingos" in Minnesota?

2.6 "Bust Amboy"

Director: George W. Brooks

Writer: Ron Friedman

SELECTED SUPPORTING CAST

Art Metrano as Amboy

Chuck Bergansky as Goose

Nicholas Worth as Denny

Richard Derr as Francis Bacon Stockwood

Lisa Mordente as Mickey

Howard Honig as Chuckles

SYNOPSIS

Threatened with a charge of harassment, Starsky and Hutch try to take down Amboy, a man with dark ambitions.

1 Q: What type of car pulls up at the funeral home?

2 Q: What does Hutch put in the bouquet of flowers?

3 Q: During the raid, in what does the chauffeur try to hide?

4 Q: Who drives during the car chase with the hearse?

5 Q: What does Starsky say is higher than his IQ?

6 Q: How old does Hutch tell Amboy's attorney Mickey is?

7 Q: To what about Mickey does Hutch draw the attorney's attention to?

8 Q: What sticks to Hutch when they go to the restaurant Starsky suggests?

9 Q: What specialty dish does Starsky recommend to Hutch?

10 Q: When Starsky and Hutch meet Amboy, which newspaper is he reading?

11 Q: Which food does Starsky mistake for possibly being grape jelly?

12 Q: What game does Hutch play with Huggy Bear?

13 Q: Where does Hutch's third dart land?

14 Q: What stings Hutch during the stakeout at Amboys?

15 Q: In the tag, what price limit does Starsky put on his snack machine offer to Hutch?

16 Q: Of what sort of business does Mickey become a field representative?

2.7 "The Vampire"

Director: Bob Kelljan

Writers: Michael Grais and Mark Victor

Speaking of vampires, Bob Kelljan also directed the 1970 film *Count Yorga, Vampire* and *Scream Blacula Scream* (1973.)

David Soul would later star in the 1979 made-for-TV movie *'Salem's Lot.*

Writers Grais and Victor went on to co-write *Poltergeist* (1982.)

SELECTED SUPPORTING CAST

G.W. Bailey as Slade

Suzanne Somers as Linda Offenbecker

John Saxon as René Nadsy

Frank Corsentino as Supergnat

Paula Sills as Suzette Clark

Lindsay Bloom as Jane

Colleen Camp as Bobette

G.W. Bailey would also appear in "The Avenger" (4.7).

Among other work, John Saxon co-starred in 1973's *Enter the Dragon* and later *A Nightmare on Elm Street* (1984).

Paula Sills would appear in "Discomania" (4.1).

SYNOPSIS

Starsky and Hutch look for a killer who makes his crimes look like the work of a vampire.

1 Q: What color are the candles around the painting of Nadsy's late wife, Maria?

2 Q: What article of clothing does Nadsy put on before leaving his house?

3 Q: What is the name of the dance club?

4 Q: Who owns the Play Pen?

5 Q: What is in the snack bowl that Starsky knocks out of Hutch's hand?

6 Q: What hits Starsky in the face when he speaks to Dobey on the payphone?

7 Q: What sort of chairs are used at Slade's Cave?

8 Q: Who mentions Hutch has a sister?

9 Q: What kind of dance does Nadsy's school teach?

10 Q: According to Starsky's reading, which wood is best for stakes?

11 Q: What does Starsky start to wear around his neck?

12 Q: What specialized item is Huggy selling in this episode?

13 Q: How many feet does Hutch say Nadsy "flew" between the buildings?

14 Q: How many students does Nadsy say he has?

15 Q: Who stands in the path of Slade's car to stop him?

16 Q: According to Slade, what kind of blood does he use in his rituals?

17 Q: Who finds Maria's photo at Slade's?

18 Q: What is Nadsy doing onstage before Linda enters?

19 Q: In the tag, where does Hutch tell Huggy he left the lizard tongues?

20 Q: What Halloween novelty is Starsky wearing at the freeze-frame?

2.8 "The Specialist"

Director: Fernando Lamas

Writer: Robert Earll

SELECTED SUPPORTING CAST

Joel Fabiani as Alexander Drew

Melendy Britt as Janice Drew

Charles Cyphers as Arthur Cole

Linda Scruggs as Officer Sally Hagan (as Linda Scruggs-Bogart)

SYNOPSIS

When two officers are killed, the suspect is a man Starsky and Hutch learn was a government agent.

1 Q: What is Hutch doing when we first see him?

2 Q: How many bombs were used on Mac's car?

3 Q: What two things does Alex Drew do to change his appearance?

4 Q: What is the name of the business Starsky and Hutch visit to find Flashy Floyd?

5 Q: What do they use to pin Flashy to the wall?

6 Q: What is the business name on the van Dobey and Cole travel in to take Starsky and Hutch to the motel?

7 Q: What is their room number?

8 Q: What is Hutch doing to occupy his time in the room?

9 Q: In the restaurant, what nickname does Starsky give to Cole?

10 Q: Who is their server?

11 Q: How does Hutch request his steak to be done?

12 Q: Where does Drew tell Hutch to meet him?

13 Q: In the tag, what two reasons does Sally give Starsky and Hutch for tossing them to the floor?

2.9 "Tap Dancing Her Way Right Back into Your Hearts"

Director: Fernando Lamas

Writer: Edward J. Lasko

SELECTED SUPPORTING CAST

Deveren Bookwalter as Carl Starger

Veronica Hamel as Marianne Tustin

Liam Sullivan as A.C. Chambers

Sondra Currie as Marsha Strearns

Audrey Christie as Ginger Evans

Dorothy Shay as Claire Dodsman

Veronica Hamel would appear in "Hutchinson for Murder One" and would later find fame on TV's *Hill Street Blues*.

SYNOPSIS

The guys go undercover to expose a blackmail operation at a dance studio.

1 Q: What is Hutch holding when he enters the dance studio?

2 Q: What does Hutch say you should do if you've "got it"?

3 Q: What does Starsky use to distract one of the gunmen at the market?

4 Q: What does Miss Tustin think Starsky's job is at the dance studio?

5 Q: As Ramon, what country does Starsky say he's from?

6 Q: For how much money do Starger and Chambers extort from Mrs. Dodsman?

7 Q: What is the name of the mouse that wins at Huggy Bear's Mouse Downs?

8 Q: How much money does Chambers try to extort from Hutch/Charlie?

9 Q: What sort of vehicle crashes into Starsky and Hutch's cab at the docks?

10 Q: How many squad cars respond to Starsky's call?

11 Q: Who fires at the tow truck?

12 Q: What does Hutch use to capture the tow truck and its occupants?

13 Q: In the tag, who gets dipped?

2.10 "Vendetta"

Director: Bob Kelljan

Writer: Don Rene Patterson

SELECTED SUPPORTING CAST

Stefan Gierasch as Arthur Fingal Solkin

Gary Sandy as Tommy Marlowe

M. Emmet Walsh as Lloyd Herman Eckworth

Ann Foster as Abigail Crabtree

Greg Elliot as Jimmy Shannon (as Gregory Elliot)

Gary Sandy would be another supporting cast member to go on to star on *WKRP in Cincinnati.*

SYNOPSIS

Starsky and Hutch investigate a man recruiting young people to commit his crimes.

1 Q: With what does Abby tickle Hutch's nose?

2 Q: Which year does Hutch say is Jimmy's JFK half-dollar?

3 Q: What is Tommy staring at while he lies on the bed?

4 Q: By what name does the hotel manager know Jimmy?

5 Q: Who searches the bureau in Jimmy's room?

6 Q: How does Hutch greet his plants when he gets home?

7 Q: What does Starsky find in Hutch's refrigerator when Hutch tells him he has "some great new goodies" there?

8 Q: For what two teams does Starsky say Lloyd Eckworth played?

9 Q: What does Lloyd say was his lifetime batting average?

10 Q: According to Hutch, how often does Starsky have to get the "Striped Tomato" tuned up?

11 Q: What does Hutch tell Capt. Dobey Starsky did with the rat?

12 Q: Of what does Artie keep a jarful near his liquor?

13 Q: Who helps Artie with his jacket?

14 Q: What does Tommy put on when he enters Abby's hallway?

15 Q: What musical knock does Tommy use at Abby's door?

16 Q: Who notices the half dollar coin at Abby's?

17 Q: Who kicks in Artie's door?

18 Q: In the tag, what does Hutch say is Abby's favorite cheese?

19 Q: What kind of cards does Starsky use for his magic trick?

2.11 "Nightmare"

Director: Randal Kleiser

Writer: Michael Fisher

SELECTED SUPPPORTING CAST

Gerrit Graham as Nicholas John Manning

Zachary Lewis as Robert 'Mousey' Loomis

Karen Morrow as Mitzi Graham

David Knapp as Asst. D.A. Jason Sims

Diana Scarwid as Lisa Graham

Carl Weathers as Al Martin

Rocky would open in theatres the month following the original air date of this episode, propelling Carl Weathers into the public eye as Apollo Creed.

Zachary Lewis would appear again in "Moonshine" (4.5).

SYNOPSIS

Starsky and Hutch must help a young mentally challenged girl after she is assaulted and raped.

1 Q: In the opening scene, for how long does Starsky say the toy store has been in that location?

2 Q: What is the name of the toy store Starsky grew up with?

3 Q: How do Starsky and Hutch travel to the 211 at the Laundromat?

4 Q: What does Hutch carry into the Laundromat?

5 Q: Aside from his holster, what is Starsky wearing when he enters the Laundromat?

6 Q: With what is Starsky playing at Discount Toys?

7 Q: According to Capt. Dobey, what is the saying about soft-hearted cops?

8 Q: What is the name of Huggy Bear's pet store?

9 Q: What is the name of the used car dealer Huggy talks about?

10 Q: What does Starsky throw across Dobey's office after Sims leaves?

11 Q: Who arrests Mousey?

13 Q: In the tag, what are Starsky and Lisa playing with?

14 Q: What addition has been made to Lisa's family?

2.12 "Iron Mike"

Director: Don Weis

Writers: (Teleplay) Ron Friedman and Arthur Norman

(Story) Arthur Norman

SELECTED SUPPORTING CAST

Michael Conrad as Capt. Mike Ferguson

Ric Mancini as Johnny Lonigan

Peter MacLean as Matt Coyle

Shannon Wilcox as Laura Lonigan

Marc Alaimo as 'Skinny' Momo

Peter MacLean would show up again in "Class in Crime" (3.17) and "Targets Without a Badge Parts 1-3" (4.18-20).

SYNOPSIS

A beloved police captain may have criminal ties.

1 Q: Starsky tells Hutch he's met a gourmet where?

2 Q: After colliding with a waiter, by what does Starsky get dragged back into the kitchen by Hutch?

3 Q: Who do they speak to after seeing Iron Mike with Coyle?

4 Q: What is the name of Coyle's business?

5 Q: A portrait of which US president does Coyle have in his office?

6 Q: When meeting with Huggy Bear at his scooter, which article of clothing does Starsky take from him to put on himself?

7 Q: When climbing the fence, who is boosted up on whose back and head?

8 Q: To which Old West lawman does Hutch compare Iron Mike?

9 Q: What is the number in the snitch book that Iron Mike tells them to call?

10 Q: In which city was Coyle really born?

11 Q: According to Coyle, what is Ferguson's Law?

12 Q: On what is Starsky reclining when Huggy tells him and Hutch the location of Laura Lonigan?

13 Q: What sort of buy does Johnny Lonigan tell them is going down that night?

14 Q: In the tag, what game are they playing?

15 Q: What is Starsky's Law?

2.13 "Little Girl Lost"

Director: Earl Bellamy

Writer: Benjamin Masselink

SELECTED SUPPORTING CAST

Kristy McNichol as Molly Edwards

Matt Bennet as Flent

King Moody as Nicholas Allen Edwards

Richard Dimitri as Duran

Guillermo San Juan as Kiko Ramos

Rebecca Balding as Officer Perkowitz

Rebecca Balding would also appear in "Class in Crime" (3.17).

As Molly is also referred to alternately as "Pete", her character is referred by whichever name is used in the scene in question.

SYNOPSIS

Recently orphaned Molly "Pete" Edwards needs Starsky and Hutch's help when her father's criminal friends come looking for her.

1 Q: On which hand does Molly wear her baseball glove?

2 Q: During what holiday season does the story take place?

3 Q: What kind of stuffed animal is dangling from the Gran Torino's rearview mirror?

4 Q: What does Hutch say he's getting Starsky for Christmas?

5 Q: What religious symbol is on the dash of the car?

6 Q: What does Molly tell them is her street address?

7 Q: Which song is Starsky whistling as they walk her to her hotel room?

8 Q: How many shots are fired at Nick?

9 Q: For what does Pete ask Hutch for breakfast?

10 Q: What does Starsky bring to Hutch's?

11 Q: What does Molly say she should have brought to the cemetery?

12 Q: To what event does Hutch think Molly would probably enjoy going?

13 Q: As what does Duran disguise himself when going to Mrs. Williams'?

14 Q: What three names does Hutch give for Santa's reindeer?

15 Q: Who is waiting with Molly at Hutch's?

16 Q: What is Hutch doing while Molly pretends to take a bath?

17 Q: Where does Molly finally find clothes she likes?

18 Q: Who alters Pete's new pants?

19 Q: Who fights with Flent?

20 Q: Where has Molly stashed the diamonds?

21 Q: In the tag, what gift does Kiko say Starsky gave to Hutch?

22 Q: Who distributes the gifts from under the tree?

23 Q: What gift is Starsky expecting from Hutch?

24 Q: What does Hutch give him?

2.14 "Bloodbath"

Director: Paul Michael Glaser

Writer: (Teleplay): Ron Friedman

(Story): Christopher Joy and Wanda Coleman

This would be the first of five episodes directed by Glaser. The others would include "Class in Crime" (3.17), "Deckwatch" (3.22), "Ballad for a Blue Lady" (4.14), "Sweet Revenge" (4.22).

SELECTED SUPPORTING CAST

Aesop Aquarian as Simon Marcus

Anthony James as Luke

Frank Doubleday as Matthew

John Horn as Peter

Patricia Pearcy as Gail Harcourt

James Brown as R.J. Crow

Raymond Allen as Merl 'The Earl'

William Bowers as Judge Yager

SYNOPSIS

Starsky is kidnapped by the followers of a crazed cult leader.

1 Q: Where have Simon's followers gathered in support of him?

2 Q: What does Hutch tell Merl the Earl not to make his car look like?

3 Q: What is Starsky's superstitious habit before a court sentencing?

4 Q: What does the note say that the bailiff hands to the judge, then to Hutch?

5 Q: What does Hutch find written on the men's room mirror?

6 Q: According to Simon, when does he dream his dreams?

7 Q: Where does Simon tell Hutch to begin his search?

8 Q: What kind of floor is the bound Starsky thrown onto?

9 Q: How many of Simon's followers are in the old storefront?

10 Q: What is in the Jack in the Box that Hutch finds in Starsky's car?

11 Q: According to Mr. Crow, what animal was killed?

12 Q: What does Starsky put on after escaping his bonds?

13 Q: What animal does Starsky face in the cave?

14 Q: Who is helping Hutch and Dobey in the captain's office?

15 Q: Who first mentions the connection to the zoo?

16 Q: What does Huggy say as Hutch and Dobey leave the office?

17 Q: In the tag, what reason does Merl give for Hutch's car being surrounded by trash?

18 Q: What part of Hutch's car has Merl refurbished, much to Hutch's chagrin?

2.15 "The Psychic"

Director: Don Weis

Writer: Michael Mann

SELECTED SUPPORTING CAST

George Loros as Earl Pola

Cliff Emmich as Marshall 'Moo-Moo' Caifano

Herb Voland as Joe Haymes

Allan Miller as Joe Collandra

Sylvia Anderson as Charlie Sireen

James Hong as Su Long

Michael Keenan as DeMeo

Edward James Olmos as Julio Gutierez

Dianne Kay as Joanna Haymes (as Diane Kay)

Edward James Olmos would go on to another Michael Mann TV show, *Miami Vice,* as well as appear in the 2003 reboot of *Battlestar Galactica.* His films would include *American Me* and *Selena.*

Allan Miller would appear in the episodes "A Body Worth Guarding" (3.14) and "Cover Girl" (4.11).

A fan favorite episode, and one of the best in the series overall.

SYNOPSIS

Starsky and Hutch turn to a psychic for help in a kidnapping case.

1 Q: Who are Starsky and Hutch chasing at the start of the episode?

2 Q: Who catches up with him at the fence?

3 Q: What is Starsky holding in his mouth while he removes the lid on his soda?

4 Q: According to Hutch, in what city was the case on which Collandra helped?

5 Q: How many kids are stealing the tires from Starsky's car?

6 Q: Where does Huggy say that Collandra said they could find "pretty dead horses" doing what?

7 Q: Who wants to check the amusement park?

8 Q: For what does Starsky ask from Hutch before opening the van's rear door?

9 Q: What business is advertised on the van in which Joanna is being held?

10 Q: What is the name of the football team owned by Joe Haymes?

11 Q: Who points out that the carwash is across from the Turbos' office?

12 Q: Who tells Joe Haymes, "There's always hope"?

13 Q: What police code does Collandra have a vision of while talking to Starsky and Hutch?

14 Q: Who trips over a chair while pursuing the robber at the bar?

15 Q: What color and make is the motorcycle used by Starsky?

16 Q: What sort of footwear does Starsky change into?

17 Q: What is Hutch's second destination during the run?

18 Q: How long is he given to get there?

19 Q: What color is Starsky's motorcycle helmet?

20 Q: What type of business is the third place Hutch must go?

21 Q: How long is he given to make it there?

22 Q: By what name does Earl Pola refer to himself when Hutch speaks to him on the laundromat's phone?

23 Q: What type of business is the fourth stop?

24 Q: How long does he have to get there?

25 Q: How many men accost Hutch in the alley?

26 Q: Who shoots Hutch?

27 Q: What is Hutch's answer to the police officer who asks, "Who are you guys?"

28 Q: Which article of clothing belonging to Joanna does Hutch give to Collandra?

29 Q: Who sees the rose painted on the side of the van before it's to be crushed?

30 Q: In the tag, what stage name has Huggy given himself?

31 Q: What does Starsky point out to Huggy about getting his and Hutch's orders mixed up?

2.16 "The Set-Up, Part 1"

Director: George McCowan

Writer: Joe Red Moffly

SELECTED SUPPORTING CAST

Jon Korkes as Terry Nash

Heather MacRae as Debra

Darrell Zwerling as Mr. Thistleman (as Darryl Zwerling)

Eugene Roche as Dr. George Stegner

Michael V. Gazzo as Joe Durniak

Bruce M. Fisher as Trucker

Darrell Zwerling would also have an appearance in "Huggy Bear and the Turkey" (2.20.).

Bruce M. Fisher would also be seen in "Moonshine" (4.5).

SYNOPSIS

A conspiracy is behind the slaying of an underworld figure.

1 Q: What is the name of the restaurant in the opening scene?

2 Q: How many men fire into Terry's car?

3 Q: What name does Terry wake up screaming?

4 Q: According to George, for how long has Terry been unconscious?

5 Q: What is the name of the cab company whose car picks up Terry?

6 Q: What is Starsky's CB handle?

7 Q: What handle does Starsky give to Hutch?

8 Q: Where is Hutch keeping his part of the $10 bill?

9 Q: For how long does Hutch tell Joe Durniak he and Starsky have been partners?

10 Q: Who paid for the funeral for Starsky's dad?

11 Q: How many bombs does Dobey say may be in the hotel?

12 Q: Who insists the bombs are a trick?

13 Q: What does Joe want inscribed on his tombstone?

14 Q: Where do Starsky and Hutch meet Terry?

15 Q: What is Terry's apartment number?

16 Q: What is the name of the Catholic Girls School Terry insists was once a hospital?

17 Q: Who gets the idea to review the security camera footage from the bank?

18 Q: What is the name of the woman being shown the slide of Terry with Starsky and Hutch?

2.17 "The Set-Up, Part 2"

Director: George McCowan

Writer: Joe Reb Moffly

SELECTED SUPPORTING CAST

Jon Korkes as Terry Nash

Heather MacRae as Debra

Darrell Zwerling as Mr. Thistleman (as Darryl Zwerling)

Eugene Roche as Dr. George Stegner

Roger E. Mosley as The Baron

Roger E. Mosley would become known as another pilot, Theodore 'TC' Calvin, in TV's *Magnum, P.I.* He would also turn up again in another role in "Huggy Can't Go Home" (4.17).

SYNOPSIS

Starsky and Hutch use the services of The Baron to help close Terry Nash's case.

1 Q: How often does Thistleman say the security cameras take a picture?

2 Q: Who first figures out that there are frames missing from the film?

3 Q: How does Terry prove he really was at the hospital-turned-school?

4 Q: What kind of bomb detonates Debra's car as well as Starsky's?

5 Q: According to Capt. Dobey, where was the rifle that killed Joe Durniak found?

6 Q: At the bowling alley, what does Starsky use to obscure his face from police?

7 Q: What does Starsky do to persuade Thistleman to respond to Hutch's instructions?

8 Q: Where does Thistleman say the castle is located?

9 Q: What is the tail number of The Black Baron's plane?

10 Q: Who mentions that flying may not have been the right idea?

11 Q: What food does Starsky ask if The Black Baron has in his bag?

12 Q: To whom does The Black Baron give the grappling hook and rope?

13 Q: Who is the first to incapacitate a castle guard?

14 Q: At what is the man in the second room looking?

15 Q: How many guns is Starsky holding when the shootout in the hallway starts?

16 Q: Who shoots down the helicopter?

17 Q: How does Capt. Dobey refer to The Black Baron?

2.18 "Survival"

Director: David Soul

Writer: Tim Maschler

SELECTED SUPPORTING CAST

Tom Clancy as Sonny McPhearson

Val Bisoglio as James Balford

John Quade as Vic Humphries

Katharine Charles as Carla Iverson

Robert Emhardt as Harry Trask

Robert Sutton as Roy Slater (as Robert Raymond Sutton)

This is the first of three episodes directed by Soul. The others are "Manchild on the Streets" (3.11) and "Huggy Can't Go Home" (4.17).

Robert Sutton would appear later in "Satan's Witches" (3.16).

SYNOPSIS

Hutch is trapped under his car when he is forced off a mountain road.

1 Q: In the opening scene, what does Bigelow give to Hutch instead of the transmitter?

2 Q: Who is first given the transmitter?

3 Q: On which hand does Starsky wear a pinky ring?

4 Q: While undercover as Scanlon, what brand of car does Hutch drive?

5 Q: How many squad cars follow the Gran Torino to assist Hutch?

6 Q: What is Hutch's one-word response to Starsky's question of how many fingers he sees?

7 Q: At the station, what is Hutch holding against his head?

8 Q: By what nickname does Balford use to refer to Starsky and Hutch?

9 Q: What does Hutch do accidentally while chopping vegetables?

10 Q: Where does Lou Scobie tell Hutch to meet him?

11 Q: What song is Sonny singing when Hutch calls to him?

12 Q: Where does Sonny think he is?

13 Q: What instrument is being tuned at The Pits?

14 Q: What part of Carla does Starsky notice is injured?

15 Q: Where does Carla say Slater is holed up?

16 Q: By what name does Hutch know the dispatcher?

17 Q: In which sector does Sonny tell Starsky Hutch is located?

18 Q: How many telephone poles does Sonny say there are from the bridge to where he found Hutch?

19 Q: In the tag, what is written in the dust of Hutch's "new" car?

20 Q: What does Hutch say about the car?

2.19 "Starsky's Lady"

Director: Georg Stanford Brown

Writer: Robert Earll

Viewers would recognize Georg Stanford Brown as Officer Terry Webster on *The Rookies.*

SELECTED SUPPORTING CAST

Season Hubley as Terry Roberts

Sanford Smith as Woody the Magic Man

Stephen McNally as George Prudholm

Rita George as Christine

Beulah Quo as Dr. Quo

Joey Vera as Freddie

It may interest readers to note that actor Joey Vera would become the bassist for heavy metal bands Armored Saint, Fates Warning, and Anthrax.

SYNOPSIS

George Prudholm returns to Bay City for revenge.

1 Q: In what game are Starsky and Hutch participating in the opening scene?

2 Q: Who is the first to suspect Terry's shooting was personal?

3 Q: What is Terry's room number at the hospital?

4 Q: Who lets himself into Hutch's place?

5 Q: The fingerprint from which digit ties Prudholm to the shooting?

6 Q: What kind of flowers does Starsky give to Terry before proposing?

7 Q: What does Terry say she's always wanted to try?

8 Q: As Starsky and Hutch approach Prudholm's door, who has their weapon drawn?

9 Q: What is Prudholm's apartment number?

10 Q: Who notices the door is booby-trapped?

11 Q: What game are the couples playing at Hutch's?

12 Q: At miniature golf, what color are Hutch's pants?

13 Q: What does Starsky tell Terry he's going to do?

14 Q: What color is Hutch's bumper car?

15 Q: Which ride does Terry say she wants to go on?

16 Q: In the hospital, how does Terry respond when Starsky tell her he loves her?

17 Q: Who drives a motorcycle through the door?

18 Q: In the tag, in which room are Starsky and Hutch playing Monopoly?

19 Q: With which football team is Hutch on the phone?

20 Q: What are the only things Starsky owns in the game?

21 Q: At what hour does the clock chime?

22 Q: What is Terry's gift to Starsky?

23 Q: What is her gift to Hutch?

24 Q: What is its name?

2.20 "Huggy and the Turkey"

Director: Jack Starrett (as Claude Ennis Starrett Jr.)

Writer: Ron Friedman

SELECTED SUPPORTING CAST

Dale Robinette as J.D. 'Turkey' Turquet

Emily Yancy as Foxy Baker

Richard Romanus as Sonny Watson

Carole Cook as 'Scorchy'

LaWanda Page as Lady Bessie (as La Wanda Page)

R.G. Armstrong as 'Dad' Watson

Fuddle Bagley as Walter T. Baker

Joe La Due as Yank

Blackie Dammett as Sugar (as Blackie Dammet)

Mickey Morton as Moon

Darrell Zwerling as Man (as Darryl Zwerling)

Fuddle Bagley would appear in "Manchild on the Streets" (3.11).

LaWanda Page would also appear in "Targets Without a Badge Parts 2 and 3" (4.19 and 4.20) and an uncredited appearance in "Starsky and Hutch on Voodoo Island" (3.1). Viewers would be familiar with her work as Aunt Esther Anderson on *Stanford and Son*.

Blackie Dammett would show up again in "Murder Ward" (3.4) and "Dandruff" (4.8). He was also the father of Red Hot Chili Peppers vocalist Anthony Kiedis.

This episode would have the dubious distinction as being the lowest-rated episode in the show's four seasons.

SYNOPSIS

Huggy Bear and J.D. 'Turkey' Turquet go into the private investigator business.

1 Q: In the opening scene, who is disguised as an old lady?

2 Q: Where does Hutch tell Foxy where she can find Huggy and the Turk?

3 Q: What game are Huggy and Turquet playing when Foxy finds them?

4 Q: What is Huggy's last name?

5 Q: From where does Huggy say Blind Bessie gets her racing tips?

6 Q: What make of car does Turquet drive?

7 Q: From what country does Bessie say Walter wanted a passport?

8 Q: What appliance does Leotis bring into the office?

9 Q: What is the signal Leotis uses to tell Huggy he's ready?

10 Q: What does Leotis do to distract Milo and Sugar?

11 Q: What do Huggy and Turquet do to break away from Milo and Sugar?

12 Q: Under what cover are Starsky and Hutch when Huggy Bear calls them?

13 Q: Whose photo is being used for reference by Hutch?

14 Q: What is Starsky holding in his teeth when Huggy calls?

15 Q: What is Hutch's cover ID?

16 Q: What is Starsky's cover ID?

17 Q: In which fruit's shape are Hutch's sunglasses?

18 Q: What does Leotis drop on Big Daddy's son and his men?

19 Q: With which hand does Turquet fire the gun?

20 Q: What rhetorical question does Starsky ask after firing a warning shot?

21 Q: In the tag, what year and kind of coin has been stolen?

22 Q: How much is it worth?

2.21 "The Committee"

Director: George McCowan

Writer: Robert I. Holt

SELECTED SUPPORTING CAST

Alex Rocco as Lt. Fargo

John Ashton as Paul H. Willits

Michael MacRae as Ward Billings

Tony Young as Officer Williams

William Cort as Officer Knight

Angela May as Ginger

William Bogert as Samuel Garner, Esq.

Muffi Durham as Millie

William Cort as Officer Knight

Alex Rocco would appear in "The Plague, Part 1" (3.8) and "The Plague, Part 2" (3.9).

William Cort would pop up again in "Moonshine" (4.5).

SYNOPSIS

Starsky and Hutch investigate a group of cops who have become vigilantes.

1 Q: In the opening scene, what is Huggy selling to Starsky?

2 Q: What game is Hutch playing?

3 Q: What does Nellie say one of Huggy's rocks did?

4 Q: Who loses Billings at the warehouse?

5 Q: From which restaurant does Hutch get their dinner?

6 Q: What does Hutch get for Starsky at Moon Café?

7 Q: Who tells them Billings was killed?

8 Q: Where does Starsky speculate sarcastically that Willits is going when they tail him?

9 Q: Who shoots Willits?

10 Q: How many uniformed cops are watching Starsky and Hutch fight at Nellie's?

11 Q: How many times does Starsky strike Hutch?

12 Q: What is Dobey eating at Hutch's place when they discuss Ginger?

13 Q: Where do Starsky and Ginger have dinner?

14 Q: What nickname does Dobey give to Fargo?

15 Q: What does Starsky throw to distract Fargo in the tunnel?

16 Q: In the tag, what has Dobey recommended Starsky and Hutch receive?

2.22 "The Velvet Jungle"

Director: Earl Bellamy

Writer: Parke Perine

SELECTED SUPPORTING CAST

Biff McGuire as Sterling

Jorge Cervera Jr. as Paco Ortega

Cliff Osmond as Harry Wheeling

Sheila Lauritsen as Laura Stevens

Silvana Gallargo as Andrea Guiterrez

Timothy Carey as Danny

Belinda Balaski as Ginny

Roberto Rodriguez as Miguelito (as Robert Rodriguez)

SYNOPSIS

Starsky and Hutch investigate a murder in the garment district when they uncover a smuggling ring.

1 Q: Who drives past the murderer in the opening scene?

2 Q: How many cartons of milk are on the tray Dobey is carrying in the hall?

3 Q: Who holds Dobey's tray?

4 Q: Who falls into a dumpster while searching the neighborhood?

5 Q: What does Brownly ask after Hutch identifies himself?

6 Q: By what name does Laura call Starsky?

7 Q: Who coaches Starsky in Spanish?

8 Q: What instruments are the musicians in the bar playing?

9 Q: What alerts Starsky, Hutch, and Ortega to trouble in Andrea's apartment?

10 Q: How many shots does Wheeling fire at Starsky and Hutch before Ortega holds him at gunpoint?

11 Q: Ortega tells Sterling to meet him at the Convention Center by what structure?

12 Q: What famous comedian is Starsky disguised as?

13 Q: What instrument is Hutch's mime "playing"?

14 Q: In the tag, who inspects the lining of Starsky's suit?

15 Q: What is Hutch's answer for why Starsky is wearing a blue shoe?

2.23 "Long Walk Down a Short Dirt Road"

Director: George McCowan

Writer: Edward J. Lasko

SELECTED SUPPORTING CAST

Lynn Anderson as Sue Ann Grainger

Joshua Bryant as Jerry Tabor (as Josh Bryant)

Dick Haynes as Cal Claybourne

Scatman Crothers as Fireball

Ben Gerard as Engineer

Lynn Anderson would be known to audiences for her version of the hit song "Rose Garden."

SYNOPSIS

Starsky and Hutch protect a popular country singer stalked by someone from her past.

1 Q: What is the name of the bar Sue Ann is performing in?

2 Q: What does Starsky ask Hutch if he's impersonating?

3 Q: What dollar amount is Tabor seeking from Sue Ann?

4 Q: Who types Sue Ann's police report?

5 Q: Who asks for an autograph from Sue Ann?

6 Q: What kind of vehicle does Tabor steal?

7 Q: What is the name of the song Sue Ann is recording?

8 Q: What was the cause of Tabor's scratchy voice?

9 Q: Who is playing catcher in Fireball's imaginary game of base-ball?

10 Q: According to Fireball, who is on base and who is batting?

11 Q: Which base does Fireball say Mantle has already stolen?

12 Q: In which hotel is Tabor staying?

13 Q: What does the hotel manager say is Tabor's room number?

14 Q: Which cab company does the manager say he called for Tabor?

15 Q: Who is first into the warehouse?

16 Q: When escaping the warehouse with Sue Ann, whose car does he take?

17 Q: In the tag, who is in the audience singing along with Sue Ann?

18 Q: Who gets up to sing with Sue Ann's band?

19 Q: By what stage name does Sue Ann refer to Hutch?

20 Q: Which nickname does Starsky call out to Hutch?

21 Q: What does Hutch do at the foot of the stage stairs?

22 Q: What is the name of Hutch's song?

2.24 "Murder on Stage 17"

Director: Earl Bellamy

Writer: Benjamin Masselink

SELECTED SUPPORTING CAST

Chuck McCann as Wally Stone

Jeff Goldblum as Harry Markham

Rory Calhoun as Steven Hanson

Layne Britton as 'Shotgun' Casey

It may interest fans to learn Layne Britton worked on 88 episodes of the show as Makeup Artist.

Jeff Goldblum would go on to success in blockbusters with acclaimed roles in *The Fly (1986)*, *Jurassic Park*, among others.

SYNOPSIS

Starsky and Hutch go undercover to track down the killer of members of an actor's exclusive club.

1 Q: What is Wally's first disguise?

2 Q: Over how many years does Steve say there have been four fatal accidents?

3 Q: What is the studio's name?

4 Q: What is the name club Steve formed with his friends?

5 Q: Who from the cast of Charlie's Angels does Starsky think he sees on the set?

6 Q: What color is Shotgun's clothing?

7 Q: What names does Shotgun refer to Starsky and Hutch?

8 Q: What happened to Hutch when he climbs the stairs of the set?

9 Q: Who almost falls through the breakaway railing?

10 Q: What is the line Hutch is given to say?

11 Q: What is the name of the water company that delivers to the studio?

12 Q: In Dobey's office, who has their feet on his desk while they're eating?

13 Q: What condiment does Dobey accuse them of getting all over the files?

14 Q: Who serves as Steve's stunt double?

15 Q: What does Ruth serve when Starsky and Hutch visit her?

16 Q: Down which street does Steve have to walk to meet Wally?

17 Q: To what classic Western does Starsky make a reference when Steve is walking?

18 Q: Which film of Wally's do Starsky and Hutch talk to him about?

19 Q: Who tells Wally he hasn't missed any of his pictures?

20 Q: To whom did critics compare Wally?

21 Q: In the tag, how many people are watching Steve's film in the screening room?

22 Q: What three things is Hutch wearing to disguise himself?

23 Q: Which relation of Hutch's did he tell about his appearance in the movie?

24 Q: Who gives Hutch the film of his missing scene?

2.25 "Starsky and Hutch Are Guilty"

Director: Bob Kelljan

Writer: David P. Harmon

SELECTED SUPPORTING CAST

Val Avery as Capt. Ryan

Lauren Tewes as Sharon Freemont

Michele Carey as Nikki

Jeanie Bell as Kate (as Jean Bell)

Shera Danese as Judith Coppet

Gary Epper as Hanson

Mary Jo Catlett as Fifi

Michele Carey would appear in "Class in Crime" (3.17).

Gary Epper was also David Soul's stunt double.

Lauren Tewes would come to be known by viewers from her stint as cruise director Julie McCoy on the hit show, *The Love Boat*.

SYNOPSIS

Starsky and Hutch are being framed by crimes committed by their doubles, right down to the Gran Torino.

1 Q: Where does Capt. Ryan sit when meeting with Starsky and Hutch in Dobey's office?

2 Q: What is Mrs. Marlowe holding when Starsky and Hutch speak to her at the diner?

3 Q: What is Hanson doing to occupy his time in the motel room?

4 Q: What is Simmons doing in the motel room?

5 Q: For how long does Dobey say he has been on the force?

6 Q: What is the name of Hutch's housekeeper?

7 Q: What Peanuts character is on Fifi's sweatshirt?

8 Q: Who does Mr. Klemp state he thought would hit him?

9 Q: On what is Hutch chewing when he and Starsky speak to the nurse?

10 Q: In what league does Starsky say Oscar Newton bowls?

11 Q: When they are disguised as a custodian, who is wearing a radio around their neck?

12 Q: Whose police record do they find in Ryan's office?

13 Q: What physical differences does Hutch note in his double?

14 Q: In the tag, what song does Starsky enter his house singing?

15 Q: For how many months does Starsky say he's been waiting for the Fats Domino record?

16 Q: What of Hutch's has been stolen?

SEASON THREE

3.1 "Starsky and Hutch on Voodoo Island"

Director: George McGowan

Writer: Ron Friedman

SELECTED SUPPORTING CAST

Samantha Eggar as Charlotte

Don Pedro Colley as Papa Theodore

Craig Stevens as Walter Healy

Roscoe Lee Browne as Quatraine

Louis Nye as Jerry

Dave Madden as Phil Hill

Jinaki as Minnie

Tommy Madden as Phillipe

Joan Collins as Janice

Paul Picerni as Johnny Doors

Anitra Ford as Silky

Patti McGuire as Pussycat (as Patricia L. McGuire)

Daina House as Easy (as Dana House)

Lane Allan as William Thorne

Linda Thompson as Meghan

LaWanda Page as Minnie (uncredited)

The cast is riddled with great character actors, not the least of which is Craig Stevens from TV's *Peter Gunn,* and Joan Collins who would star on the hit series, *Dynasty.*

SYNOPSIS

Starsky and Hutch investigate the murders and strange occurrences on a millionaire's tropical island.

1 Q: What is the name of the club they go into in the first scene?

2 Q: What creature does Starsky mention as being spotted at Pine Lake?

3 Q: At the SLOBS gathering, what kind of pattern is Starsky's jacket?

4 Q: What is their flight number?

5 Q: To what does Janice compare Thorne's house security?

6 Q: At the airport, who between Starsky and Hutch is wearing shorts?

7 Q: What color are Starsky's socks?

8 Q: Who is their driver from the airport?

9 Q: How many guards are at the main entrance of Thorne's estate?

10 Q: How many bags is Hutch missing?

11 Q: Thorne's estate is up against which hole of the golf course?

12 Q: On which hand does Hutch wear his golfing glove?

13 Q: How many guards with dogs catch Starsky and Hutch on Thorne's estate?

14 Q: Outside of his aunt's house, how does Huggy tell them to walk?

15 Q: Who is a walking display for hats and necklaces?

16 Q: Who meets them in the steam room?

17 Q: Who is revealed to be the mastermind behind the conspiracy against Thorne?

18 Q: Who first sees the dead boar hanging outside their room?

19 Q: What does Huggy Bear say is the wrong side of the bed?

20 Q: Who does Starsky attack on the trail to Thorne's?

21 Q: Who collapses and fakes an occult seizure after getting captured by Baron?

22 Q: Who sees "the big green voodoo bird"?

23 Q: How many people in total escape in the convertible?

24 Q: How much money does Charlotte promise to the one whomever "brings them down"?

25 Q: How does Janice lose her gun?

26 Q: What does Hutch use as an improvised weapon against their pursuers?

27 Q: Who rescues them after Starsky jumps the car into the water?

28 Q: In the tag, what does Starsky say will be the movie on the flight home?

29 Q: What does Janice put in her hat, then abruptly discards after the revelation of Papa Theodore's escape?

3.2 "Fatal Charm"

Director: Earl Bellamy

Writer: Jeff Kanter

SELECTED SUPPORTING CAST

Karen Valentine as Diana Harmon

Roz Kelly as Officer Linda Baylor

Paul Lukather as Max Frost

Janice Heiden as Kathy Marshall

The role was a significant departure for Karen Valentine, who was known for wholesome roles.

SYNOPSIS

Hutch's new love interest becomes obsessed with the detective.

1 Q: Who pursues the purse snatcher in the opening scene?

2 Q: What does Starsky use as an improvised ladder during the chase?

3 Q: Which hand does Hutch injure?

4 Q: What does Starsky give to Hutch before leaving the exam room?

5 Q: In what does Starsky get his hand stuck?

6 Q: Where does Hutch have a key secreted away?

7 Q: What is Diana making when Hutch finds her in his apartment?

8 Q: What story does Diana say she told the apartment manager?

9 Q: What gift does Diana buy for Hutch?

10 Q: What is the inscription Diana has put on the watch?

11 Q: What does Hutch do when he first sees his trashed apartment?

12 Q: What one word does he say about the smashed guitar?

13 Q: What is Starsky doing when Hutch tells him about what happened?

14 Q: Who criticizes Hutch on the location of the key to his apartment?

15 Q: What does Huggy have to do to find Hutch's phone?

16 Q: Who is operating a jackhammer?

17 Q: Who attaches the cable to Frost's car?

18 Q: In the tag, which condiment does Hutch recommend for Linda's hospital food?

19 Q: What gift does Capt. Dobey bring?

20 Q: How much does Dobey say it'll cost to repair the damage to the sidewalk?

3.3 "I Love You, Rosie Malone"

Director: Rick Edelstein

Writer: Tim Maschler

SELECTED SUPPORTING CAST

Tracy Brooks Swope as Rosey Malone

John P. Ryan as Frank Malone

James Keach as Ed Chambers

Paul Jenkins as Bill Goodson

John Dullaghan as Ray Shelby

Mary Mercier as Secretary

Mary Mercier would show up again in "Black and Blue" (4.9) and be seen in 1980's feature film, *Airplane!*

SYNOPSIS

An undercover Starsky falls for the daughter of a mobster.

1 Q: What are Starsky and Hutch doing in the opening scene?

2 Q: What is the word on Rosie's shirt when Starsky joins her jogging?

3 Q: Which legendary basketball player does Hutch say Starsky is not?

4 Q: Where do the guys meets Goodson and Chambers?

5 Q: Whose name does Starsky mispronounce intentionally?

6 Q: What is Hutch's parting shot to Chambers and Goodson before leaving the office?

7 Q: Starsky tells Rosie he likes which classical composer?

8 Q: Starsky first tells Rosie he does what for a living?

9 Q: What color is Starsky's bedroom phone?

10 Q: Who kicks in the door at Shelby's place?

11 Q: What does Rosie say after learning from her father Starsky's a cop?

12 Q: What drink does Starsky prepare for Rosie while she's in the shower?

13 Q: At Goodson's office, who does Hutch slam up against a wall?

14 Q: What does Frank Malone think will happen to his operation once he retires?

15 Q: Where is Rosie's dad waiting while she and Starsky talk alone?

16 Q: What does Starsky do after he and Rosie say goodbye.

17 Q: In the tag, what does Hutch ask Starsky if he's taking?

18 Q: What does Starsky say is the first part of his diet?

3.4 "Murder Ward"

Director: Earl Bellamy

Writer: Anthony Yerkovich

SELECTED SUPPORTING CAST

Suzanne Somers as Jane Hutton

Joey Forman as Freddie Lyle

Fran Ryan as Miss Bycroft

Leon Charles as Dr. Matwick

Ned York as Switek

Blackie Dammett as Charlie Deek

Vincent Schiavelli as Weeze

SYNOPSIS

Starsky goes undercover as a patient and Hutch as an orderly at an asylum to investigate several deaths.

1 Q: Who is brought into the institution in a straitjacket?

2 Q: What song does he hum?

3 Q: Who does Starsky literally run into in the hall?

4 Q: For how long has Hutch been working there undercover?

5 Q: Who does Starsky spot also working undercover?

6 Q: What does Bo do after offering a chair to Starsky?

7 Q: What poker game does Weeze offer Starsky to play?

8 Q: What is Starsky holding when he talks to Freddie in the parking lot?

9 Q: Who is providing commentary at the cockroach race?

10 Q: What is the name Starsky has given to the races?

11 Q: Nurse Bycroft kills which roach?

12 Q: Not including the corpse of the Cabrillo Kid, what is Starsky holding before he's sedated?

13 Q: What accessory does Hutch-as-Hansen wear on the ward?

14 Q: Which two books does Hutch give to Starsky?

15 Q: According to Freddie, what color and make of car does Switek drive?

16 Q: After Switek's murder, who wants to pull the plug on the investigation?

17 Q: In whose room does Jane stash the newspaper clipping?

18 Q: What food of Hutch's does Matwick drug?

19 Q: Who releases Starsky, saying "It's gone too far"?

20 Q: Who saves Hutch from Charlie Deek?

21 Q: How many shots does Matwick fire at Starsky?

22 Q: How does Hutch stop Matwick?

23 Q: In the tag, which song are the patients singing?

24 Q: What is Jane dressed as?

25 Q: What name does Jane's nametag read?

26 Q: Whose birthday do they end up celebrating?

3.5 "Death in a Different Place"

Director: Sutton Roley

Writer: Tom Bagen

SELECTED SUPPORTING CAST

Don Gordon as Lt. Alec Corday

Gregory Rozakis as Nick Hunter

Art Fleming as John Blaine

Rick Davalos as Orrin Lawford (as Dick Davalos)

Charles Pierce as 'Sugar'

Virginia Laith as Margaret Blaine

SYNOPSIS

Starsky and Hutch investigate the death of a senior officer to discover compromising circumstances.

1 Q: How many blocks away does Hutch say the station is from where they've stopped?

2 Q: For how many days in a row does Hutch say Starsky's car has broken down?

3 Q: Into what bar does John go?

4 Q: What is John's room number?

5 Q: In the Squad Room, what does Hutch hold close to his face?

6 Q: What is the name of the hotel where John stayed?

7 Q: Whose car is used to pursue Nick?

8 Q: How does Nick explain the money in his pocket?

9 Q: What does Nick wear around his neck on a chain?

10 Q: What is Lawford making on his stove?

11 Q: What is Lawford's room number?

12 Q: What is Sugar doing when Nick comes to his house?

13 Q: What does Corday shoot, thinking it's Nick?

14 Q: Who does Corday take hostage?

15 Q: During the standoff with Corday, who is wearing a hat and sunglasses?

16 Q: In the bar during the shootout, over what musical instrument does Starsky jump for cover?

17 Q: Over what does Hutch jump for cover?

18 Q: Starsky counts how many shots from Corday's gun?

19 Q: On whom does Corday land after Hutch punches him?

20 Q: Who questions Starsky's count of bullets shot?

21 Q: In the tag, which car are they driving?

22 Q: Where is Starsky seated?

3.6 "The Crying Child"

Directors: Georg Stanford Brown

Randal Kleiser (opening scene, uncredited)

Writer: James Schmerer

SELECTED SUPPORTING CAST

Dee Wallace as Carol Wade

Linda Dano as Janet Mayer

Rosalind Cash as Sgt. Sheila Peterson

Meeno Peluce as Guy Mayer

Mike Lane as Eddie Mayer (as Michael Lane)

Jason Ronard as Coop

Nancy McKeon as Vikki Mayer

Al White as Franklin

Dee Wallace went on to memorable roles in films such as *E.T. the Extra-Terrestrial, Cujo,* and *The Howling.*

Nancy McKeon found a starring role in TV's *The Facts of Life.*

Franklin White would go on to act in memorable scenes in the comedy film, *Airplane!*

Author's note: The entire opening sequence is lifted from "Nightmare" (2.11).

SYNOPSIS

The guys find themselves in an investigation involving an abused child.

1 Q: What famous comedy duo are they dressed as on their way to rehearsal?

2 Q: Which baseball team's hat does Guy wear?

3 Q: During their rehearsal, what does Starsky do with his shoe?

4 Q: Where does Dobey note Starsky and Hutch were to go on their two-day leave?

5 Q: What does Janet Mayer do for a living?

6 Q: What two jobs does Starsky say are the only two that Franklin has had?

7 Q: Who shoulder-tosses Eddie to the ground?

3.7 "The Heroes"

Director: Georg Stanford Brown

Writers: Kathy Donnell and Madeline DiMaggio Wagner

SELECTED SUPPORTING CAST

Karen Carlson as Christine D. Phelps

Jerrold Ziman as Paul Rizzo

Lynn Borden as Roxy

Madison Arnold as Karl Regan

Lee McLaughlin as Al O'Riley

SYNOPSIS

The guys have a newspaper writer along with them to research an article she is writing.

1 Q: What is Hutch reading when they enter the Squad Room?

2 Q: At the deli, what does Tony have in his mouth?

3 Q: What do they pretend to see when Tony doesn't cooperate?

4 Q: In addition to a notebook, what else does Chris use?

5 Q: What does Starsky ask for from Roxy?

6 Q: What does Starsky do with his drink when Larry the Fall Guy is on the ground?

7 Q: What astrological sign is Chris?

8 Q: How many cigarettes does Starsky light for the smokers in the bar?

9 Q: In the article, what nickname does Chris use for them?

10 Q: In the tag, who is driving?

11 Q: What is Chris's next article titled?

12 Q: When Hutch sees the house Starsky has put a deposit on, what does he say is the only way the house can be fixed?

13 Q: What is Hutch's response when his partner insists the house has potential?

14 Q: What is being used as the house's front steps?

15 Q: What happens when Hutch tries to walk on it?

3.8 "The Plague, Part 1"

Director: Bob Kelljan

Writer: William Douglas Lansford

SELECTED SUPPORTING CAST

Janet Margolin as Dr. Judith Kaufman

Frank Marth as Dr. Meredith

Jean Allison as Helen Yeager

Al Ruscio as Roper

Alex Rocco as Thomas Callendar

Patrick Labyorteaux as Richie Yeager (as Patrick Laborteaux)

Paul Kent as Lt. Anderson

Walter Matthews as Lt. Jake Donner

Natalie Norwick as Virginia Donner

SYNOPSIS

It's a race against time when Starsky has to find a hitman, the only man in the city who can help a dying Hutch and possibly the city from a contagious virus he has survived.

1 Q: For how many years does Hutch say he wants to live?

2 Q: Who goes first through the airport metal detector?

3 Q: At what time is Jake's plane to arrive?

4 Q: What does the thief in the airport throw in Starsky's path?

5 Q: What happens to Starsky's car outside the airport?

6 Q: Callendar gets into what color taxi?

7 Q: What does Callendar claim to do for a living?

8 Q: Where is Jake when he collapses?

9 Q: Who takes Virginia Donner to the doctor's office?

10 Q: What business does Big Benny have?

11 Q: Callendar's rifle is missing which part?

12 Q: How much does Callendar pay for the firing pin?

13 Q: Where does Starsky tell Hutch the thermos of coffee is located in the car?

14 Q: What is Callendar disguised as when Starsky and Hutch tail Roper?

15 Q: In which branch of the service did Starsky serve?

16 Q: For what does the disguised Callendar ask from Roper's driver?

17 Q: What gives Callendar's disguise away to Hutch?

18 Q: How many shots total does Callendar fire at both Roper and Starsky and Hutch?

19 Q: Who almost gets hit by the car Callendar escapes in?

20 Q: In how many hours does Dr. Meredith say Hutch will manifest symptoms?

21 Q: How many days do they have to find the antitoxin?

22 Q: How does Hutch refer to the wheelchair they bring in for him?

3.9 "The Plague, Part 2"

1 Q: Which part of Hutch does Dr. Kaufman say is vulnerable?

2 Q: What kind of magazines does Hutch tell Meredith he's finished reading?

3 Q: What does Starsky tell Huggy he'll hock if it would help find Callendar?

4 Q: When observing a rapidly deteriorating Hutch, for what does Starsky ask from Dr. Kaufman?

5 Q: What does Hutch wake to see written on his window?

6 Q: How old is the Scotch Callendar bought?

7 Q: What does Starsky tuck into his waistband before knocking on Helen's door?

8 Q: What superhero does Starsky tell Hutch he'll be like after they find the serum he needs?

9 Q: Who argues against Starsky's idea of using the media to find Callendar?

10 Q: What game is Roper playing when Starsky goes to see him?

11 Q: How many bodyguards are in the room with Roper and Starsky?

12 Q: What is Dobey carrying when he goes to visit Hutch?

13 Q: What phone number does Dr. Kaufman give on the air?

14 Q: Roper tells his men to cover which two places?

15 Q: How much money does Callendar tell the cab driver he'll get if he cooperates?

16 Q: Behind what does Starsky take cover during the shootout at the hospital?

17 Q: To whom does Callendar say, "I owe you one"?

18 Q: In the tag, Starsky tells Hutch he's not ready for what?

3.10 "The Collector"

Director: Ivan Nagy

Writer: Don Rene Patterson

SELECTED SUPPORTING CAST

Robert Viharo as Jack Gallagher/Jack Cunningham

Toni Kalem as Molly Bristol

Danny DeVito as John 'John John the Apple' DeAppoliso

Susan Tyrell as Annie/Isabelle Oates

Dave Shelley as Lee Bristol

Richard Le Pore as Frank Carroll

Marki Bey as Officer Minnie Kaplan

Roberto Rodriguez as Mike Todasco

Danny DeVito would find fame in his role as TV's Louie De Palma on *Taxi*.

Marki Bey would reappear as Officer Minnie Kaplan in the episodes "The Avenger" (4.7), "Cover Girl" (4.11), "Birds of a Feather" (4.15), "Ninety Pounds of Trouble" (4.16), and "Starsky vs. Hutch" (4.21).

SYNOPSIS

The guys find that there's a new debt collector is in Bay City.

1 Q: Hutch notes that Mr. Bristol used to play with whom?

2 Q: What color is the flower in Gallagher's lapel?

3 Q: According to the sign outside of Annie's, her dogs are trained to do what?

4 Q: How many dogs does Annie actually have?

5 Q: Starsky tells Hutch not to do what to his car?

6 Q: What does Annie claim that her dog can smell?

7 Q: Hutch says Annie is rumored to keep her fortune where?

8 Q: What does Gallagher do to Mr. Carroll's toilet?

9 Q: Hutch notes that Annie started her acting career at what age?

10 Q: What is the name of Huggy's bar?

11 Q: What fear does Annie have?

12 Q: Which of Huggy Bear's licenses does Hutch say is expired?

13 Q: What does Gallagher bring for Ducha the next time he visits?

14 Q: Who objects to bringing Molly into undercover work?

15 Q: John the Apple reminds a customer to take her what?

16 Q: Who IDs Gallagher?

17 Q: In what does Gallagher say he escaped the convent?

18 Q: What does Gallagher rub over his gun before going up to Annie's?

19 Q: When reclining on Annie's bed, what besides a drink is Gallagher holding?

20 Q: How many shots does Hutch fire at Gallagher?

21 Q: Which parts of his body does Gallagher say are broken?

22 Q: Which of them affects an Irish accent when arresting Gallagher?

23 Q: In the tag, what did a drunken Mr. Bristol do after dropping his gun in a sewer?

24 Q: What does Starsky speculate happened to Bristol's gun?

25 Q: What condiment does Hutch put on Starsky's pastrami?

3.11 "Manchild on the Streets"

Director: David Soul

Writers: (Teleplay) Rick Edelstein

(Story) Steve Fisher

SELECTED SUPPORTING CAST

J. Jay Saunders as Jackson Walters

Sheila Frazier as Dr. Sammie Mason

Dorothy Meyer as Mrs. Walters

Fuddle Bagley as Dewey

Helen Martin as Vivian Fellers

Shizuko Hoshi as Mrs. Hong

Maurice Sneed as Maurice

Maurice Sneed was later in "Black and Blue" (4.9).

SYNOPSIS

The son of a friend of Starsky and Hutch plots revenge when his father is killed.

1 Q: What game is being played at the start of the episode?

2 Q: Who finds the bag of pills dropped by Junior?

3 Q: What does Jackson do for a living?

4 Q: Who goes to talk with Junior after his confrontation with his father?

5 Q: Which part of Dewey's car is hanging off?

6 Q: What is the call sign of the cops who pursue Dewey and Jackson?

7 Q: Who watches what Hutch is typing as he fills out a report?

8 Q: What does Maurice take from behind the bar at the pool hall?

9 Q: What does Junior take from Sammie's purse?

10 Q: At the hospital, Junior and Maurice are disguised as what?

3.12 "The Action"

Director: Ivan Nagy

Writers: (Teleplay) Alvin Friedman (as Al Friedman) and Robert E. Swanson (as Robert Swanson)

(Story) Alvin Friedman (as Al Friedman)

SELECTED SUPPORTING CAST

Carmine as Sam Eberly

Richard Venture as Clay Hilliard

James Sikking as Ted McDermott

M. Emmet Walsh as Freddie

Melanie Griffith as Julie McDermott

John Carradine as The Professor

Quin Cummings as Toni McDermott

Melanie Griffith would be nominated for an Academy Award for Best Actress for *Working Girl*.

The prolific John Carradine would end up with 354 acting credits in his career.

Quinn Cummings would join Kristy McNichol on *Family*.

SYNOPSIS

Starsky and Hutch go undercover as high rollers in an underground gambling operation.

1 Q: What is the name of Hilliard's club?

2 Q: What sports game is being broadcast in the first scene in the club?

3 Q: What penalty does Starsky announce when Toni tackles Hutch?

4 Q: On what part of Starsky does Hutch say he caught frostbite seven years before?

5 Q: To whom does Ellen reveal Ted's gambling problem?

6 Q: How much flash money does Dobey give them?

7 Q: Huggy places a bet on which horse?

8 Q: In what position does the horse first finish the race?

9 Q: By what alias does the Professor say Joseph Nolan is under?

10 Q: Undercover at the club, what does Hutch say the name of Gene Autry's horse was?

11 Q: What does Julie slip down Starsky's shirt?

12 Q: Who teaches them how to switch dice?

13 Q: Who switches the dice in the second game?

14 Q: Who starts the fight at the game?

15 Q: Who refuses to dig his own grave?

16 Q: In the tag, what two things does Hutch tell Ted that Freddie is getting back in addition to his money?

17 Q: What card game is Starsky playing with Toni and Julie?

18 Q: What does Starsky throw in the air in a comical bluster when he loses?

3.13 "The Heavyweight"

Director: Earl Bellamy

Writers: (Teleplay) Robert E. Swanson

(Story) Norman Borisoff

SELECTED SUPPORTING CAST

Gary Lockwood as Jimmy Spenser

Shaka Cumbuka as Booker Wayne

Bernard Behrens as Haley Gavin

Susan Buckner as Sharon Carstairs

J.R. Miller as Stevie Spenser

Whitman Mayo as Jeeter

SYNOPSIS

A boxer gets tangled up in the world of crooked boxing.

1 Q: Where does Starsky tell Hutch he fell asleep on his date the night before?

2 Q: Jeeter compares Jimmy to which real-life boxer?

3 Q: Who is Jimmy fighting?

4 Q: In which round does Gavin tell Jimmy to go down?

5 Q: Who takes Starsky's popcorn?

6 Q: To where is Sharon flying in the morning?

7 Q: Into which hotel does Huggy say Jimmy is?

8 Q: Who says Jimmy is washed up as a fighter?

9 Q: How much money does Gavin tell Jeeter he'll be paid if he cooperates?

10 Q: Who tells Jimmy that Jeeter is helping Gavin?

11 Q: Who gets to the warehouse first, Starsky or Hutch?

12 Q: In the tag, where does Jimmy say he and his wife might move?

13 Q: What news does Sharon give?

14 Q: What does Starsky do with Hutch's beer?

3.14 "A Body Worth Guarding"

Director: Rick Edelstein

Writers: (Teleplay) Sam Paley and Rick Edelstein

(Story) Sam Paley

SELECTED SUPPORTING CAST

Monique van de Ven as Anna Akhanatova

Michael Margotta as Miller

Signe Hasso as Masha Barovnika

Allan Miller as Morty Kaufman

SYNOPSIS

A romance develops between a Russian ballet dancer and Hutch that he and Starsky are assigned to protect.

1 Q: To which ballet company does Anna belong?

2 Q: Starsky says Anna has more moves than what famous boxer?

3 Q: What word does Hutch call out repeatedly at the end of the performance?

4 Q: Who has trouble pronouncing Anna's last name?

5 Q: After test firing the gun at a standee of Anna, what does Miller say needs adjusting?

6 Q: What secret does Anna tell Hutch?

7 Q: What physical display does Hutch do that Anna copies?

8 Q: What does Anna tell Hutch their child would look like if they had one?

9 Q: In what sport do Hutch and Anna compete?

10 Q: After pulling his gun on the bellman, of what candy does Hutch tell him the gun is made?

11 Q: What Russian word does Anna ask Hutch to repeat?

12 Q: By what name does Anna refer to Starsky?

13 Q: How does Anna pronounce "Hutch"?

14 Q: What song does Hutch perform for Anna?

15 Q: When he and Masha go to Hutch's how does Starsky know Hutch is home?

16 Q: How many shots does Miller fire at Anna?

17 Q: Who tackles Miller?

18 Q: In the tag, to what does Anna challenge Starsky to a game of?

3.15 "The Trap"

Director: Earl Bellamy

Writers: (Teleplay) Sidney Green (as Sid Green) and Robert E. Swanson (as Robert Swanson)

(Story) Sidney Green (as Sid Green)

SELECTED SUPPORTING CAST

Kristy McNichol as Joey Carston

Bill McKinney as Johnny Bagley

Pat Morita as Jewelry Store Owner

Antony Ponzini as Trayman

Anthony Geary as Delano

Ann Prentiss as Mrs. Carston

Pat Morita would be known to audiences as a TV staple on shows like *Happy Days.* Later, he would star in *The Karate Kid* (1984).

Anthony Geary would star in the soap opera *General Hospital* as Luke Spencer.

Ann Prentiss would reprise the role of Mrs. Carston in "Ninety Pounds of Trouble" (4.16).

SYNOPSIS

When Starsky and Hutch are lured into a trap, they realize young Joey Carston has come along for the ride.

1 Q: What is the make and model of the watch bought by Starsky?

2 Q: What is the number on Joey's jersey?

3 Q: What does Starsky crash into while chasing Joey?

4 Q: What kind of store does Joey run through to lose Starsky and Hutch?

5 Q: Who were the thugs who beat up Huggy looking for?

6 Q: When Starsky and Hutch spot Joey on the street, who follows her on foot?

7 Q: What did Joey steal?

8 Q: Where does Joey stow away in Starsky's car?

9 Q: What part of the car does Joey keep banging her head against?

10 Q: How long does Bagley give Hutch to think about his situation?

11 Q: From where does Joey get her idea of how to escape?

12 Q: To which actor does Joey compare Starsky?

13 Q: Where does Starsky get shot?

14 Q: Whose idea is it to use the tractor?

15 Q: What car did Starsky's Uncle Alfonse have?

16 Q: What does Hutch pour into the tractor?

17 Q: What does Starsky give to Hutch?

18 Q: In the tag, who comes out of Dobey's office with the captain?

19 Q: Into whom does Starsky fall when Hutch kicks his cane out from under him?

3.16 "Satan's Witches"

Director: Nicholas Sgarro

Writer: Bob Barbash

SELECTED SUPPORTING CAST

Charles Napier as Sheriff Joe Tyce

Taylor Lacher as Hank Ward

Robert Sutton as Cabot (as Robert Raymond Sutton)

Joseph Ruskin as Rodell

SYNOPSIS

A weekend trip to the mountains brings danger to Starsky and Hutch.

1 Q: Whose car do they take to the cabin?

2 Q: What color is Rodell's robe?

3 Q: What is the name of the lake?

4 Q: After being awoken by Hutch's singing, what does Starsky throw at him?

5 Q: Who notes the symbol on the cabin door is written in blood?

6 Q: When they speak to Julie and Trisha, what does Hutch say is the closest Starsky gets to the woods?

7 Q: Where does Trisha plant the rattlesnake?

8 Q: Who finds the snake?

9 Q: When they speak with Sheriff Tyce, by what nickname does Hutch refer to Rodell?

10 Q: What does Hutch run his car into accidentally?

11 Q: What does Starsky say when discovered by one of Rodell's men outside of where Lizzie is held?

12 Q: Back at the Dobey cabin with Lizzie, what game does Starsky suggest in order to deal with Rodell's men?

13 Q: What question does Starsky ask the invaders after he shakes a maraca?

14 Q: With what does Hutch hit the last henchman?

15 Q: In the tag, what is Starsky doing?

16 Q: What do they hear that changes Starsky's mind about staying?

3.17 "Class in Crime"

Director: Paul Michael Glaser

Writer: Don Rene Patterson

SELECTED SUPORTING CAST

Peter MacLean as Professor Gage

Rebecca Balding as Mickie Marra

Michele Carey as Catlin

Carl Anderson as Ralph

SYNOPSIS

A college professor commits crime using his unique philosophy.

1 Q: In the first scene, what part of Mickie as a mime first comes into frame?

2 Q: What rifle component does Mickie tell Gage he left in the van?

3 Q: Who is the first to inspect the rifle Gage left behind?

4 Q: For what show does Gage say Jack Morgan is a fanatic?

5 Q: What does Hutch tell Starsky to do with his badge when it fails to make an impression on Catlin?

6 Q: Who walks past Starsky and Hutch when they're parking outside of Jack's apartment?

7 Q: What sort of questions does Gage say he does not ask?

8 Q: Who is at Gage's house when Starsky investigates?

9 Q: From whom is the framed note on Gage's wall?

10 Q: What three things does Mickie tell Starsky to do when she figures him for a cop?

11 Q: What does Ralph say the writer of the note on the blackboard loses if they go to the police?

12 Q: What does Gage tell Mickie the signal will be for her to shoot Hutch?

13 Q: In the tag, how long does Starsky say it'll take for Hutch to pay for his new rod and reel?

14 Q: Who ends up with a fishing net over their head?

3.18 "Hutchinson for Murder One"

Director: Bob Kelljan

Writers: (Teleplay) Robert E. Swanson (as Robert Swanson)

(Story) Jackson Gillis (as Sid Green)

SELECTED SUPPORTING CAST

Veronica Hamel as Vanessa

Floyd Levine as Boyle

Alex Courtney as Officer Simonetti

Bill Duke as Officer Dryden

Dan Vadis as Cardwell

SYNOPSIS

Hutch's ex-wife is murdered, and he's the prime suspect.

1 Q: Vanessa and Hutch meet where?

2 Q: For what does Hutch ask from Huggy Bear?

3 Q: What is Vanessa's drink?

4 Q: Where does Vanessa stash the pouch?

5 Q: What drink does Starsky pour for Hutch after she's found murdered?

6 Q: What is Hutch's blood type?

7 Q: Who slugs Simonetti?

8 Q: Who finds the pouch in Hutch's car?

9 Q: Who first speculates that Vanessa was working with Wheeler?

10 Q: To what does Dryden end up handcuffed?

11 Q: What does Starsky do with Dryden's gun before giving it back to him?

12 Q: To what kind of business does Starsky arrange for the diamond to be brought?

13 Q: In what is Huggy Bear hiding?

14 Q: Who knocks out Wheeler?

15 Q: In the tag, for how much does Starsky say he paid for Louise?

16 Q: As what kind of animal does Dobey properly identify Louise?

3.19 "Foxy Lady"

Director: Nicholas Sgarro

Writer: Robert E. Swanson (as Robert Swanson)

SELECTED SUPPORTING CAST

Morgan Woodward as Clay Zachary

Mark Gordon as John Carelli

Priscilla Barnes as Lisa Kendrick

Darrell Zwerling as Stu Basset

Priscilla Barnes would later be cast in *Three's Company.*

SYNOPSIS

A witness to murder with stolen money has her own plans for it.

1 Q: What falls out of its box when Hutch removes it from the fridge?

2 Q: About what does Starsky tell Lisa Hutch's neighbors complain?

3 Q: How does Hutch wake Starsky the following morning?

4 Q: For what does Starsky dive onto the bed?

5 Q: Where does the note end up?

6 Q: To what destination does Hutch discover Lisa has a ticket?

7 Q: How much does Maggie say Lisa paid for her clothes?

8 Q: When he finds Zachary and Carelli ransacking his house, what does Hutch throw at Zachary?

9 Q: In which coat pocket does Hutch have the handcuff key?

10 Q: Who jumps on Zachary's back when the fight breaks out?

11 Q: In what does Zachary try to escape?

12 Q: What does Starsky tell Hutch is really in the suitcase?

13 Q: In the tag, how much does Lisa get from the bank as a reward?

14 Q: What does Lisa leave with Starsky and Hutch?

3.20 "Partners"

Director: Charlie Picerni (as Charles Picerni)

Writer: Rick Edelstein

Picerni would also direct "Birds of a Feather" (4.15).

SELECTED SUPPORTING CAST

Ralph Nelson as Dr. Greene

Kathleen King as Marsha Henry

Melissa Steinberg as Bonnie Ackerman

Zacharie Lewis as Henderson (as Zachary Lewis)

Ronnie B. Baker as Billy Joe

SYNOPSIS

When Hutch seems to have amnesia following a crash in the Gran Torino, Starsky tries to jog his memory.

1 Q: In the opening scene, Hutch is talking about "the sweet sounds of" what?

2 Q: During the chase, what does Starsky tell Hutch not to do in his car?

3 Q: What kind of vehicle do they crash into?

4 Q: What does Starsky yell when he sees the empty hospital bed next to his?

5 Q: How does an "amnesiac" Hutch pronounce Starsky's name?

6 Q: What card game has Hutch allegedly forgotten?

7 Q: How does Hutch pronounce Dobey's name?

8 Q: What does Hutch ask sarcastically about Huggy Bear?

9 Q: Huggy tells Hutch that he and Starsky go back farther than whom?

10 Q: By what alias is Huggy paged over the PA?

11 Q: What name that Starsky mentions gives Hutch pause in his ruse?

12 Q: At what game does Hutch tell Starsky he gets stomped?

13 Q: In the tag, for what does Dobey tell the guys to report in the morning?

14 Q: What does he tell them to bring?

3.21 "Quadromania"

Director: Rick Edlestein

Writer: Anthony Yerkovich

SELECTED SUPPORTING CAST

Richard Lynch as Lionel Fitzgerald II

John McLiam as Lionel 'Gramps' Fitzgerald Sr.

Phillip Michael Thomas as Kingston St. Jacques

Lynne Marta as K.C. McBride

Susan Kellermann as Monique (as Susan Kellerman)

Susan Kellerman would appear in "Black and Blue" (4.9).

Philip Michael Thomas would later find fame in the hit TV show, *Miami Vice*.

SYNOPSIS

Starsky goes undercover as a cabbie to catch the murderer killing taxi drivers.

1 Q: To what does Carboni compare with the killer's grip?

2 Q: What game is set up in front of Gramps when we first see him?

3 Q: For what play does Lionel "read" a review of aloud to Gramps?

4 Q: What does Kingston toss to Hutch before getting the trip sheets?

5 Q: What does KC keep in the backseat of her cab?

6 Q: Where is the taxi stand Hutch tells Starsky to check as much as possible?

7 Q: What game does Starsky play with Gramps when he and Hutch question him?

8 Q: What does Gramps throw at Hutch when he investigates a closed door?

9 Q: Where was Lionel hiding during the visit from Starsky and Hutch?

10 Q: What is Lionel disguised as when he gets into Starsky's cab?

11 Q: How many times does Starsky note he's driven the disguised Lionel around the park?

12 Q: Who drives Hutch to Starsky's location?

13 Q: In the tag, with whom is Starsky dancing?

14 Q: Who shows up as KC's manager?

3.22 "Deckwatch"

Director: Paul Michael Glaser

Writer: Don Rene Patterson

SELECTED SUPPORTING CAST

Michael Baseleon as Hector Salidas

Kathryn Harrold as Laura Kanen

Susan French as Hannah Kanen

Carole Mallory as Madelaine

Will Walker as Chicky

Will Walker would reprise the role of Chicky in "The Groupie" (4.10).

SYNOPSIS

A wounded killer takes shelter in the home of Hutch's friend, holding her and her mother hostage.

1 Q: With which caliber gun did Madeline shoot Hector?

2 Q: Where on his body is Hector wounded?

3 Q: What does Chicky lend to Hector?

4 Q: At Laura's house, for how much rum does Hector tell her to get for him?

5 Q: By what name does Hector tell Hannah he prefers to be called?

6 Q: For how long does Dobey give Hutch to be in the house disguised as a paramedic?

7 Q: Where does Hutch strap on his gun before going into the house?

8 Q: What color eyes does Hannah note Hector as having?

9 Q: Of what does Hutch tell Hector he's sick of seeing?

10 Q: How many "stages" does Hutch use as a countdown for Starsky to make his move?

11 Q: In the tag, what kind of pie has Laura made for Hutch?

12 Q: Who gets hit with the pie?

SEASON FOUR

4.1 "Discomania"

Director: Arthur Marks

Writer: Rick Edelstein

SELECTED SUPPORTING CAST

Pierrino Mascarino as Tony Mariposa

Adrian Zmed as Marty Decker

Susan Duvall as Judith

Amanda McBroom as Sgt. Lizzie Thorpe

Tom Tarpey as Harding

Debbie Chaffin as Rita (as Deb-E-Chaffin)

Paula Sills as Michelle

Adrian Zmed would later star in the TV show, *TJ Hooker*.

In 1979, Amanda McBroom's song "The Rose" would be recorded by Bette Midler and would be one of her biggest hits.

SYNOPSIS

Starsky and Hutch along with Sgt. Lizzie Thorpe go undercover at a disco to catch a serial killer.

1 Q: What is the title of the book Starsky is reading?

2 Q: Which food does Dobey tell Starsky to lay off?

3 Q: How tall does Hutch say is Lizzie's husband?

4 Q: Who keeps taking women away from Tony?

5 Q: Who puts out the APB on Lizzie?

6 Q: Who first hears the music coming from Tony's private disco?

7 Q: Who is first through the door of Tony's disco?

8 Q: What color are the candles at Tony's disco?

9 Q: In the tag, who says they're so sick and tired of discos they could scream?

10 Q: What dances does Starsky suggest he and Hutch teach Capt. Dobey?

11 Q: Who opens the door to the Squad Room while Dobey is dancing?

4.2 "The Game"

Director: Leo Penn

Writer: Tim Maschler

SELECTED SUPPORTING CAST

Jack Ging as Ray Pardee

Suzanne Charny as Gina

Liz Torres as Anita

Joseph R. Sicari as Ernie Silvers

Raymond Allen as Merl 'The Earl'

SYNOPSIS

Hutch is in danger during a bet with Starsky that he can stay hidden for 48 hours.

1 Q: What does Huggy say all worry gets you?

2 Q: For how many weeks salary is the bet?

3 Q: Who loses the pool game and has to pay the tab?

4 Q: How often does Hutch says he will check in with someone different?

5 Q: Which hotel does Hutch check into?

6 Q: Who buys a pencil from a disguised Hutch?

7 Q: Who puts the APB on Hutch?

8 Q: How many shots are fired at Starsky in The Pits?

9 Q: Who tells Hutch Starsky was shot?

10 Q: Gina tells Starsky she'd recognize Hutch even if he was wearing a mask of what monster?

11 Q: Who tells Starsky where to find Hutch?

12 Q: In the tag, Hutch is meditating on what piece of furniture?

4.3 "Blindfold"

Director: Leo Penn

Writers: Pat Fielder and Richard M. Bluel (as Richard Bluel)

SELECTED SUPPORTING CAST

Kim Cattrall as Emily Harrison

Gary Wood as Don Widdicombe

Robin Strand as Kenny Widdecombe

Kim Cattrall would become known for her work in *Sex and the City.*

SYNOPSIS

Starsky is guilt-stricken when a round from his gun accidentally blinds a young woman.

1 Q: In the opening scene, what tool is being used to open the safe?

2 Q: What percentage of crime does Starsky say occurs on Sundays?

3 Q: Who tells Hutch to let Widdecombe go?

4 Q: When he leaves his place, what does Starsky take with him instead of his gun?

5 Q: What actress does Starsky imitate while talking with Emily?

6 Q: With what musical instrument does Hutch annoy Pinky at the pawn shop?

7 Q: What game is Kenny Widdicombe playing when Hutch intrudes on it?

8 Q: What is Starsky's response when Hutch tells him he looks lousy?

9 Q: Where does Don Widdecombe tell Emily he's intending for them to go?

10 Q: On whom do Starsky and Hutch train their guns when they meet at Emily's?

11 Q: Who removes the Mars light from atop the car as they pull into the parking garage?

12 Q: When Emily's vision begins to return, who does she see?

13 Q: Who warns Starsky that Don has a gun?

14 Q: In the tag, for how long does Hutch say he could remain blindfolded?

15 Q: How many fingers does Starsky remind Hutch are used in the Boy Scout salute?

16 Q: What does a blindfolded Hutch almost immediately trip over?

4.4 "Photo Finish"

Director: Sutton Roley

Writers: (Teleplay) Robert E. Swanson

(Story) Michael I. Wagner and Robert E. Swanson

SELECTED SUPPORTING CAST

Graham Jarvis as Basil Monk

Britt Lind as Marcie Fletcher (as Brit Lind)

Shera Danese as Nicole Monk

Fran Ryan as Landlady

Lois Hamilton as Paula (as Lois Areno)

Sally Kirkland as Greta Wren/Dora Pruitt

Sally Kirkland would be nominated for the Academy Award for Best Actress for her role in the 1987 feature film, *Anna*.

SYNOPSIS

Starsky and Hutch go undercover in the circles of the well-to-do.

1 Q: In the opening scene, out of what magazine does Hutch tell Starsky he looks?

2 Q: What happens when Hutch tries to remove the tag from Starsky's jacket?

3 Q: How many rolls of film does Marcie keep for herself?

4 Q: To what animal does Nicole compare Basil?

5 Q: With what toy is Basil playing while being questioned by Starsky and Hutch?

6 Q: For how much is Dora-as-Greta Wren offering to pay for the negative rights?

7 Q: What is Reinhardt's secretary wearing on her head?

8 Q: What is the name of one of the plants outside Reinhardt's office?

9 Q: On what does Basil tell Hutch he spent the $30,000?

10 Q: To whom does Marcie tell the disguised Dora she sold the negative?

11 Q: Where does Basil hide from Dora?

12 Q: By what name does Dora refer to herself when confronting Basil?

13 Q: How many total shots does Dora fire at the toys?

14 Q: At whom does she fire her empty gun when the lights come on?

15 Q: Who handcuffs Dora to Basil?

16 Q: In the tag, what clothing do they wear to The Pits?

17 Q: What drink does Huggy Bear serve them?

18 Q: What does Starsky note Huggy forgot to remove from the bottle?

19 Q: Who gets sprayed with champagne?

4.5 "Moonshine"

Director: Reza Badiyi

Writer: Fred Freiberger

SELECTED SUPPORTING CAST

Billy Green Bush as Willy Hall

Zachary Lewis as Melvin Hall

Shug Fisher as Sam Ivers

James Noble as Treasury Agent Kendall

Mary Louise Weller as Dolly Ivers

Lee McLaughlin as Earl

Pat Corley as Ben Meadows

Bruce M. Fisher as Rudy

William Cort as Detective Hank Munson

James Noble would perhaps be best remembered for his later long-time TV role as Governor Eugene X. Gatling on *Benson*.

SYNOPSIS

The guys investigate the source of lethal bootleg booze.

1 Q: With what does Kendall say the moonshine is cut?

2 Q: Of which American Prohibition agent has Dobey never heard?

3 Q: How many presidents does Sam tell Dolly their bootlegging operation has survived?

4 Q: Dolly drives what color truck?

5 Q: When at the Smokey Mountain Inn, from which state do Starsky and Hutch say they are?

6 Q: Which of them gets so drunk they fall off their barstool?

7 Q: What does Rudy do with the card Hutch gives him?

8 Q: What part of Starsky sticks out of the car while Hutch drives?

9 Q: What alias does Hutch use?

10 Q: What does Munson say after Starsky and Hutch go roaring off with his truck?

11 Q: In which bar does Hutch perform?

12 Q: By what alias does Starsky identify himself to Dolly?

13 Q: As C.W., Hutch professes to be the hottest country picker this side of where?

14 Q: How many sacks of sugar do Starsky and Hutch haul in the pickup?

15 Q: Who pursues Willy on a motorcycle?

16 Q: In which boot does Willy carry a gun?

17 Q: What does Hutch crash into with the motorcycle?

18 Q: In the tag, who is Roxy's new dance partner?

19 Q: Which dance does Starsky tell Hutch he doesn't know?

4.6 "Strange Justice"

Director: Reza Badiyi

Writer: Rick Kelbaugh

SELECTED SUPPORTING CAST

Mary Crosby as Leslie Slate (as Mary Frances Crosby)

Juli Andelman as Lori Prescott

Susan Heldfond as Cassie

Carl Anderson as Marsellus Cobb

Kenneth McMillan as Lt. Daniel Slate

Lindsay Bloom as Officer Dee O'Reilly

SYNOPSIS

The daughter of a veteran cop is raped and Starsky and Hutch have to make sure justice is served rather than the revenge sought by her father.

1 Q: How much does O'Reilly tell Hutch his parking ticket will cost?

2 Q: What sort of music does Cassie tell Leslie will damage her brain cells?

3 Q: What does Leslie take away from Lori?

4 Q: What number is on Lori's football jersey pajamas?

5 Q: Who gives Hutch another parking ticket?

6 Q: What does Cobb give to Slate?

7 Q: When pursued by Starsky and Hutch, into which hotel does Cobb duck?

8 Q: What is Cobb's room number?

9 Q: At which profession does Cobb tell them he's looking for work?

10 Q: Who puts the APB out on Slate?

11 Q: Who tells Hutch he's going to Slate's home?

12 Q: What rhetorical question does Starsky ask before he and Hutch move to confront Slate and Biggs?

13 Q: Who arrests Slate?

14 Q: In the tag, who does Internal Affairs say they're investigating?

15 Q: Who has a date with O'Reilly?

4.7 "The Avenger"

Director: Sutton Roley

Writer: Robert E. Swanson (as Robert Swanson)

SELECTED SUPPORTING CAST

Joanna Cassidy as Monique Travers/Harry Ashford

Tim Thomerson as Phil

Michael DeLano as Roger

G.W. Bailey as Hotel Clerk

Marki Bey as Officer Minnie Kaplan

Joanna Cassidy would act in many TV shows and films, including 1982's *Blade Runner.*

SYNOPSIS

Starsky and Hutch investigate a case of the stalker of a woman who kills the men she sleeps with.

1 Q: How old does Starsky say are the newspapers he finds inside Harry's room?

2 Q: What does Hutch find in the trash can?

3 Q: What does Hutch call the device he shows to Starsky?

4 Q: What is Monique making for Phil when she hears Harry's voice?

5 Q: At the hotel, what informal contest is taking place?

6 Q: What is Harry's room number?

7 Q: What is the name of the club on the book of matches given to them by Bobbie?

8 Q: Minnie tells Hutch she's dancing her way to what?

9 Q: What instrument does Starsky play at Monique's?

10 Q: Who does Hutch first suspect of being Harry Ashford?

11 Q: What does Monique throw across the room?

12 Q: Who tells Hutch Monique is not a redhead?

13 Q: What one word does Monique-as-Harry repeat when attacking Starsky?

14 Q: In the tag, what color are Starsky's shoes?

15 Q: What phase does Hutch tell Starsky his biorhythms still are in?

16 Q: Where does the bee sting Starsky?

4.8 "Dandruff"

Director: Sutton Roley

Writer: Ron Friedman

SELECTED SUPPORTING CAST

Rene Auberjonis as The Baron

Madison Arnold as Dinty

Blackie Dammett as Ellis

Tracey Walter as Leo (as Tracey Walters)

Jacques Aubuchon as Davidowsky

Audrey Meadows as Hilda Zuckerman

Norman Alden as Buddy Owens (as Norm Alden)

Leigh Hamilton as Vivian

F. William Parker as Harry

Rene Auberjonois would go on to success in TV's *Benson.*

Viewers would be familiar with Audrey Meadows for her performances in *The Honeymooners.*

SYNOPSIS

The guys go undercover as hairdressers to foil a mysterious jewel thief.

1 Q: What alias is Hutch using?

2 Q: What sort of exaggerated accent is used by Starsky?

3 Q: What undercover name is used by Starsky?

4 Q: Where do they end up in the pursuit of the casino robbers?

5 Q: Who rests their bare feet on Dobey's desk?

6 Q: By what name are the diamonds known?

7 Q: What is the only clue Dobey has on The Baron?

8 Q: What does Starsky use to avoid Mrs. Zuckerman seeing him?

9 Q: Of what is Starsky-as-Tyrone especially protective from Mrs. Zuckerman?

10 Q: What is the name of the man who runs the smoke shop?

11 Q: For what brand of cigar does Hutch ask him about?

12 Q: How much does Leo tell Hutch a box of Superbas cost?

13 Q: What does Starsky carry with him when he and Hutch go to deliver the cigars at the cabaret?

14 Q: How many shots from Buddy's gun does Hutch fire into the floor?

15 Q: What color is The Baron's cigar cutter and lighter?

16 Q: By what does Mr. Adachi identify himself?

17 Q: What does Davidowski call the pouch in which the diamonds are carried?

18 Q: How many diamonds are in the Belvedere Collection?

19 Q: What is The Baron disguised as when he escapes?

20 Q: Where has he hidden the stones?

21 Q: In the tag, what beauty treatment are Starsky and Hutch receiving?

22 Q: Who sends the note along with the cigars to them?

4.9 "Black and Blue"

Director: Rick Edelstein

Writer: Rick Edelstein

SELECTED SUPPORTING CAST

Vonetta McGee as Inspector Joan Meredith

René Le Vant as Lionel Train (as Rene Levant)

Candace Brown as Vivian

Lili Valenty as Mrs. Greene (as Lily Valenty)

Regina Baff as Elaine (as Regie Baff)

Susan Kellermann as Mary (as Susan Kellerman)

Mary Mercier as Nurse #1

SYNOPSIS

When Hutch is wounded, Starsky is paired with a new partner in Inspector Joan Meredith.

1 Q: In Hutch's car, what is Starsky checking?

2 Q: What color does Hutch pick for the test?

3 Q: What number does Starsky correctly predict from Hutch?

4 Q: What call sign does Starsky first give when they respond to a call?

5 Q: What does Starsky throw through the home's window?

6 Q: As Hutch is wheeled through the hospital halls, what number does he tell Starsky he was really thinking?

7 Q: What does Mrs. Greene give to Starsky while Hutch is in surgery?

8 Q: Before going into Interrogation, what does Starsky ask Meredith if she has?

9 Q: What does Meredith poke into Starsky's side during their wrestling match?

10 Q: On what does Hutch hit his head during Dobey's visit in the hospital?

11 Q: How much does Vivian give Mary for information?

12 Q: Who tells Huggy Bear that Hutch almost got killed?

13 Q: On what article of clothing does Meredith compliment Huggy?

14 Q: What does Hutch use to mime talking on the phone while Starsky talks to Huggy?

15 Q: What does Mrs. Greene tell Starsky to go do?

16 Q: Who tells Train that Vivian shot a cop?

17 Q: What reason does Starsky give to Meredith as to why he can't go undercover at Train's?

18 Q: What appliance does Vivian have to borrow from Starsky?

19 Q: Which of Hutch's arms is in a sling?

20 Q: When Hutch and Dobey get to Train's, who covers the front?

21 Q: In the tag, who gets between Starsky and Meredith as they're saying goodbye?

22 Q: What question does Starsky ask Meredith just before the freeze-frame?

4.10 "The Groupie"

Director: Nicholas Colasanto

Writer: Robert Dellinger

SELECTED SUPPORTING CAST

Caren Kaye as Melinda Rogers

Joh Ashton as Roy Sears

David Knapp as Bill Walters

Arthur Roberts as Ed Ohlin

Darryl McCullough as Harold

Marianne Bunch as Barbara Wilson

Gerald Hiken as Mr. Marks

Robert Loggia as Jack Parker

SYNOPSIS

Starsky and Hutch go undercover to foil a racketeering ring in the world of fashion.

1 Q: How many bullets does Melinda remove from Harold's gun?

2 Q: For what company does Harold work?

3 Q: When Starsky as Renaldo meets Hutch's Jack Ives, which magazine does he mention shooting for?

4 Q: Where is Jack Parker holding his "Anchors Aweigh" party?

5 Q: What is Hutch drinking when Melinda and the models are showing the swimsuits?

6 Q: When in a photo session, what does Starsky tell the model she has coming out of her nose?

7 Q: What is the name of Melinda's dog?

8 Q: From what graduating class does Hutch claim to be to Melinda?

9 Q: From how many yards does Melinda say she can read a cop?

10 Q: How much does Starsky bet Hutch on a game of eight-ball at The Pits?

11 Q: Who overhears Melinda's phone conversation with Capt. Dobey?

12 Q: On what movies does Dobey say Melinda has OD'd?

13 Q: Who does Hutch tell Parker is his designer?

14 Q: How many shots total does Parker fire at Starsky?

15 Q: Into what do Hutch, Parker, and a model fall?

16 Q: In the tag, who joins Starsky and Hutch at The Pits?

17 Q: Who is revealed to be Melinda's date?

4.11 "Cover Girl"

Director: Rick Edelstein

Writers: (Teleplay) Robert Dellinger and Rick Edelstein

(Story) Daniel B. Ullman (as Dan Ullman)

SELECTED SUPPORTING CAST

Maud Adams as Kate Larrabee

Allan Miller as James Brady

Calvin Lockhart as Allen 'Angel' Walter

Jerome Guardino as Lindsay

Jeffrey Tambor as Randy

Marki Bey as Officer Minnie Kaplan

Jeffrey Tambor would be known to modern audiences for his work in *Transparent* and *Arrested Development*.

Maud Adams had previously appeared in *The Man with the Golden Gun* and would also be in another James Bond film, *Octopussy*.

SYNOPSIS

A model with terminal cancer hires a hitman to kill her before the cancer does, then [tries to cancel when the cancer goes into remission.

1 Q: What is Hutch eating while taking the phone call from Stuart Ross?

2 Q: From where is Starsky coming when he gets to the squad room?

3 Q: With what remote controlled toy is Angel playing when Brady speaks to him at the park?

4 Q: How many doctors does Dr. Harriman say confirmed her remission?

5 Q: What game is Angel playing by himself in his hotel room?

6 Q: Over how many years does Kate ask if Hutch has thought about her?

7 Q: What does Kate say is important when death is over your left shoulder?

8 Q: What are Hutch's and Starsky's respective call signs over the walkie-talkies?

9 Q: Whose walkie-talkie sets off the bomb under Kate's car?

10 Q: Under what name did Angel purchase the remote?

11 Q: Between what two things does Angel test the light bulb bomb?

12 Q: Who suggests to Starsky to check change of address records?

13 Q: What is Angel disguised as when he plants the bomb at Kate's?

14 Q: What do Starsky and Hutch use as a pretend phone at Kate's?

15 Q: Who kicks Angel's door open?

16 Q: Who saves Kate's life?

17 Q: In the tag, who does Randy have stand next to Kate in the photo session?

18 Q: What emotion does he ask from Starsky?

4.12 "Starsky's Brother"

Director: Arthur Marks

Writers: (Teleplay) Ralph Wallace Davenport and Robert Earll

(Story) Ralph Wallace Davenport

SELECTED SUPPORTING CAST

Jack O'Leary as Victor

Nicholas Worth as Al

Eddie Fontaine as Jake

Stanley Grover as Frank Weldon

David Moss as Bronson

Elisabeth Brooks as Marlene (as Elizabeth Brooks)

Antony Ponzini as Frank Stryker

SYNOPSIS

Starsky's younger brother comes into town and trouble follows.

1 Q: In the opening scene, what does Mrs. Krupp mouth to Hutch as he leaves the room?

2 Q: What does Hutch give to Officer Sweeney before meeting with Capt. Dobey?

3 Q: What is happening to Starsky's car outside the airport?

4 Q: What is Nick's full name?

5 Q: At what club does Nick meet with Stryker?

6 Q: Who does Marlene compliment on their dancing?

7 Q: What Beatles song is Nick singing after the disco?

8 Q: Where does Starsky tell his brother to sleep?

9 Q: What does Starsky throw on Stryker's table during his phone call?

10 Q: How many years does Hutch remind Starsky it's been since he's seen Nick?

11 Q: What does Huggy Bear tell Hutch makes fools of us all?

12 Q: What excuse does Hutch give Starsky to go see Huggy alone?

13 Q: What is the name of the business Nick is being held?

14 Q: In the tag, who is taking a shot at the pool table when the scene opens?

15 Q: How much does Starsky pay out for the loss?

16 Q: For how much does Nick propose another game?

17 Q: What handedness does Starsky reveal Nick to be?

4.13 "The Golden Angel"

Director: Sutton Roley

Writers: (Teleplay) Joe Reb Moffly & Robert Dellinger and George Arthur Bloom

(Story) George Arthur Bloom

SELECTED SUPPORTING CAST

Steve Oliver as Buzzy Boone

Lynn Benisch as Candy Reese (as Lynn Benesch)

Hilary Beane as Camille Boone

Richard Karron as Hammerlock Grange

Ray Walston as Tommy Reese

Viewers at the time would have been familiar with Ray Walston's past work on TV's *My Favorite Martian.*

SYNOPSIS

The guys investigate the death threats received by a wrestler before a match.

1 Q: In which arm is Buzzy shot?

2 Q: What is the name of the firm representing Starsky's uncle's estate?

3 Q: Hutch's metaphorical "highway we call life" has how many lanes?

4 Q: Starsky refers to Tommy Reese as wrestling's answer to whom?

5 Q: What nickname does Stella give to Starsky?

6 Q: Which wrestling move does Hammerlock demonstrate on Starsky?

7 Q: What phrase does the skull in Buzzy's locker repeat over and over?

8 Q: Before a broadcast of Spotlight on Sports, with what part of his costume does Buzzy ask Hammerlock for help?

9 Q: What does Hammerlock smash during the broadcast?

10 Q: How many shots are fired through the window at Buzzy?

11 Q: What is Huggy Bear carrying in the ring when he accompanies the disguised Starsky?

12 Q: Hutch as referee takes away what weapon from Hammerlock?

13 Q: What is Hammerlock doing while Buzzy and Starsky argue in the ring?

14 Q: What does Starsky put on Hutch before leaving the ring?

15 Q: In the tag, who has paid for the party for the wrestlers?

16 Q: Huggy says Camille is the most violent what he's ever seen?

17 Q: How much money does Starsky ask from Hutch?

18 Q: What is the date on Starsky's inheritance check?

4.14 "Ballad for a Blue Lady"

Director: Paul Michael Glaser

Writer: (Teleplay) Sidney Ellis and Paul Michael Glaser

(Story) Sidney Ellis

SELECTED SUPPORTING CAST

Malachi Throne as Joe Finch

Arell Blanton as Casey O'Brien

Stack Pierce as Chicky

John Karlen as Deputy D.A. Stanton

Jenny O'Hara as Marianne Owens

SYNOPSIS

Hutch becomes involved with a blues singer with underworld ties.

1 Q: In the opening scene, who throws Stanton out of the crime scene?

2 Q: On what is the undercover Hutch writing at the bar when Marianne orders her drink?

3 Q: How does Marianne order her drink?

4 Q: From where does Marianne think Hutch is?

5 Q: Hutch tells Marianne she sounds like which two singers?

6 Q: What does Marianne lose when Hutch leads her away from Joe Fitch's men through a busy street?

7 Q: What does Starsky hold in Harry's face when Starsky wakes him?

8 Q: Who tells Harry that Hutch is a cop?

9 Q: What does Hutch tell Marianne she has to own?

10 Q: In the hallway shootout, how many shots does Hutch fire?

11 Q: In the tag, where are Starsky and Hutch?

12 Q: How many new leaves does Hutch count on a plant?

13 Q: Which singer's music does Hutch tell the plant he's going to play for it?

4.15 "Birds of a Feather"

Director: Charlie Picerni

Writers: (Teleplay) Amanda J. Green and Rick Edelstein

(Story) Amanda J. Green

SELECTED SUPPORTING CAST

Allan Arbus as Anthony Reuban

Martin Kove as Jimmy Lucas

Charles Cyphers as Detective Webster

Barbara Stuart as Doris Huntley

John P. Ryan as Detective Luke Huntley (as John Ryan)

Marki Bey as Officer Minnie Kaplan

SYNOPSIS

The wife of Hutch's former partner is in deep gambling debt to the wrong people.

1 Q: What is the name of the hotel Dobey wants to use to guard Palmer?

2 Q: What is Palmer's room number?

3 Q: How many years does Luke tell Starsky it took Hutch to make Sergeant First Class?

4 Q: With what does Starsky dry Luke's sarcastic tears?

5 Q: What does Huggy Bear tell Luke to call him?

6 Q: In the poker game, what is Doris's hand?

7 Q: Not including the lights, what two things does Doris turn on when she returns home from the game?

8 Q: What does Luke do with the payment agreement in Reuban's office?

9 Q: Who serves the warrant on Reuban?

10 Q: What item does Reuban tell Gloria to get as a present for his uncle Louie?

11 Q: Where does Doris say she's going when Hutch finds her packing?

12 Q: How much does Luke demand from Reuban in exchange for his silence?

13 Q: How many men does Reuban arrive with to meet Luke?

14 Q: Who hangs out of the driver side window of Reuban's car when he tries to escape?

15 Q: In the tag, who is playing pool with Starsky, Hutch, and Huggy?

16 Q: What does Dobey say his nickname used to be?

17 Q: What shot does Dobey call?

18 Q: What happens when he takes the shot?

4.16 "Ninety Pounds of Trouble"

Director: Leo Penn

Writer: Robert E. Swanson (as Robert Swanson)

SELECTED SUPPORTING CAST

Kaz Garas as Eddie Carlyle

Lana Wood as Sidney 'Sid' Archer

Mare Winningham as Joey Carston

Ann Prentiss as Mrs. Carston

Marki Bey as Officer Minnie Kaplan

Mare Winningham would go on to co-star in the film *St. Elmo's Fire* and numerous TV appearances.

SYNOPSIS

Joey Carston (recast with Winningham in the role) compromises an undercover operation of Starsky and Hutch's.

1 Q: In the opening scene, who pours coffee for Starsky?

2 Q: What happens to Starsky when he tries to kick in Carlyle's door?

3 Q: In which room of Chez Moi does Hutch tell Damon to meet him?

4 Q: Under what pretense does Starsky approach Sid in her booth?

5 Q: What drink does Joey order at The Pits?

6 Q: What is Hutch doing to occupy his time at the hotel when Schiller calls him?

7 Q: In the hospital, what does the real Carlyle steal from the nurse's tray?

8 Q: What does Hutch say to Sid after he shoots Starsky?

9 Q: Who tails Hutch and Damon after Starsky is shot?

10 Q: In the tag, to which concert does Starsky have tickets?

4.17 "Huggy Can't Go Home"

Director: David Soul

Writers: (Teleplay) Rick Kelbaugh

(Story) Rick Edelstein

SELECTED SUPPORTING CAST

Richard Ward as J.T. Washington

Francesca P. Roberts as Cora-Lee (as Francesca Roberts)

Lee Weaver as Boseman

Royce D. Applegate as Dolphin

Bryan O'Dell as Junior

Roger E. Mosley as Bid Red McGee (as Roger Mosley)

SYNOPSIS

Huggy Bear must help a friend regain stolen money.

1 Q: To which boxer does Lonnie compare Huggy?

2 Q: What is Monahan drinking at the poker table?

3 Q: What does Starsky get a bag of for himself and Hutch?

4 Q: What does Officer Butler spot on Hutch's moustache?

5 Q: What two cards does Hutch find up Boseman's sleeve?

6 Q: How many Fudgsicles does Starsky tell Hutch the newsboy conned him out of?

7 Q: What is Huggy doing when Starsky and Hutch go to see him at The Pits?

8 Q: What is the name of the restaurant Cora-Lee works?

9 Q: In what hotel do Dolphin and Big Red stay?

10 Q: Where is Hutch sitting when Starsky picks him up at the parking lot?

11 Q: What does Dolphin use as a weapon to threaten Big Red?

12 Q: Who knocks out Huggy Bear?

13 Q: What is Huggy holding when he later confronts Big Red?

14 Q: What does Huggy say after Hutch calls out, "Huggy, where are you?"

15 Q: In the tag, where are Starsky and Hutch having drinks with Huggy Bear?

16 Q: What does Huggy hold in the air at the freeze-frame?

4.18 "Targets Without a Badge, Part 1"

Director: Earl Bellamy

Writer: Rick Kelbaugh

SELECTED SUPPORTING CAST

Ken Kercheval as Deputy D.A. Clayburn

Robert Tessier as Soldier

Troas Hayes as Mardean Rigger

Quinn K. Redeker as Deputy Police Chief Reasoner (as Quinn Redeker)

Ted Neely as Lionel Rigger (as Ted Neely)

Peter MacLean as Judge Raymond McClellan

Ken Kercheval would become better known on the TV sensation, *Dallas.*

SYNOPSIS

A federal judge has ties to drug running and the guys resign from the force.

1 Q: In what city does the episode start?

2 Q: When we first see Starsky and Hutch, on what is Starsky chewing?

3 Q: What card does Starsky think was Hutch's?

4 Q: What sign does Hutch make when he and Starsky pull alongside the girls on the way to Los Angeles?

5 Q: What decoration does Lionel have on his drum set?

6 Q: What does Lionel say he'd be losing money on if he were in Vegas?

7 Q: What signal does Starsky give to Lionel to let him know they can hear his transmitter?

8 Q: Who first reads the letter sent to Lionel?

9 Q: What is the Evidence Code Hutch cites in court to the judge?

10 Q: Where does Lionel tell the guys he sent Mardean and Jamie?

11 Q: Who goes to speak to Dobey alone?

12 Q: Where is Hutch when the bomb is planted under his car?

13 Q: After Lionel is killed, who is the first person to reprimand Starsky and Hutch?

14 Q: Who is the second to confront them about Lionel's death?

15 Q: What item does Hutch plant in the sand on the beach?

16 Q: What do they do at the freeze-frame?

4.19 "Targets Without a Badge, Part 2"

SELECTED SUPPORTING CAST

William Prince as James Marshall Gunther

1 Q: What is Starsky kicking around in the opening scene?

2 Q: What is Hutch holding as he drives to Starsky's?

3 Q: What is the name of Hutch's car?

4 Q: At Employment Development, what does Starsky toss casually on the desk of the employee Hutch falls into?

5 Q: What does Starsky use to stop the pair fleeing on the motorcycle?

6 Q: According to Starsky, how did Laura Anderson die?

7 Q: What is the name on the van driven by the woman selling flowers?

8 Q: What is Hutch's response when Agent Smithers tells him and Starsky that they're trying his patience?

9 Q: What do they discover stolen from out of Starsky's car?

10 Q: What is the name on the tag on the officer taking their report about the car?

11 Q: In the tag, what paperwork does Starsky ask Capt. Dobey to expedite?

12 Q: What is Hutch's response when Dobey asks them, "What are you guys up to?"

4.20 "Targets Without a Badge, Part 3"

1 Q: What color suit does Mrs. Swayder tell Huggy the previous mortgage salesman wore?

2 Q: In what part of the Trojan Spa do Starsky and Hutch wait for Thomas?

3 Q: While they argue about their truck getting towed, what happens to Starsky and Hutch?

4 Q: When getting the gun permits, what type of hat is Hutch wearing?

5 Q: To what type of dashboard does Hutch say he's allergic?

6 Q: Hutch tells Starsky they walked into this case with all the finesse of what?

7 Q: What question does Hutch ask when Starsky tells Hutch he's going to exchange himself for Alison?

8 Q: During the exchange, what street does Starsky ask Alison if she remembers?

9 Q: Who is sitting behind them at the matinee?

10 Q: In the tag, what do Starsky and Hutch do with the badges given to them by the mayor?

4.21 "Starsky vs. Hutch"

Director: Peter Levin

Writer: Rick Edelstein

SELECTED SUPPORTING CAST

Richard Lynch as Joey

Topo Swope as Arlene

Yvonne Craig as Carol

William Sanderson as Weirdo (as William J. Sanderson)

Marki Bey as Officer Minnie Kaplan

Viewers would be familiar with Yvonne Craig from another TV show, *Batman,* in which she played Barbara Gordon/Batgirl.

William Sanderson would go on to act in *Blade Runner* and TV's *Newhart.*

One of the least popular and out-of-character episodes in the series.

SYNOPSIS

Starsky and Hutch compete for the affection of the same woman, a fellow police officer.

1 Q: To which fictional detective does Hutch sarcastically refer to Starsky in the opening scene?

2 Q: Who does Starsky tell Kira Hutch is supposed to be guard-ing?

3 Q: Who brings Starsky coffee in the Squad Room?

4 Q: What is Joey Webster doing while blindfolded?

5 Q: Where is Starsky sleeping when Hutch comes home?

6 Q: For how long does Starsky tell Hutch he's been seeing Kira?

7 Q: At the dance hall, what does the note on the telephone read?

8 Q: What does Starsky help put up on Kira's wall?

9 Q: What game at the dance hall does Joey ask Susan to play?

10 Q: What is the serial number Joey recites?

11 Q: What is Hutch carrying when he goes to Starsky's?

12 Q: Who does Starsky tell he's in love with Kira?

13 Q: What is the name of the dance hall?

14 Q: What game does Joey play with Kira?

15 Q: Who catches and throws the grenade Hutch kicks out of Joey's hand?

16 Q: In the tag, what drink, not including beer, do both Starsky and Hutch order from Huggy Bear?

4.22 "Sweet Revenge"

Director: Paul Michael Glaser

Writers: (Teleplay) Steven Nalevansky

(Story) Steven Nalevansky & Joe Reb Moffly

SELECTED SUPPORTING CAST

Sean P. Griffin as Jonathan Wells (as Sean Griffin)

Conrad Bachmann as Doctor (as Conrad Bachman)

Alex Courtney as Bates

William Prince as James Marshall Gunther

Ivan Bonar as Lancaster

SYNOPSIS

James Marshall Gunther returns, contracting a hit on one Dave Starsky. Hutch must strike out on his own to find Gunther while Starsky fights for his life.

Series Finale.

1 Q: What is Gunther holding in the opening scene?

2 Q: What are Starsky and Hutch playing in the Squad Room?

3 Q: Who wins the game?

4 Q: How many shots does Hutch fire at the fleeing gunmen?

5 Q: Who joins Hutch and Dobey outside of Starsky's hospital room?

6 Q: Who hands Hutch the car keys as he exits the hospital elevator?

7 Q: Whose car do the keys belong to?

8 Q: When speaking to Dobey on the phone in the Squad Room, what is Hutch bouncing on the desk?

9 Q: What is a nurse doing when Hutch tries to tell her Starsky's awake?

10 Q: A replica of what famous Rodin sculpture is on Gunther's office table?

11 Q: Who serves the coffee for Bates?

12 Q: Who does Gunther tell Hutch had been looking forward to meeting him?

13 Q: What two things does Hutch place on Gunther's desk?

14 Q: How many shots are fired during the struggle for the gun?

15 Q: In the tag, what does Hutch note is the time?

16 Q: How many painkillers does Starsky say he's taken?

17 Q: What does Hutch do with the serving tray's lid?

18 Q: What does Hutch claim to have turned an orderly into?

19 Q: What does Dobey bring?

20 Q: What does Huggy bring?

21 Q: What does Dobey tuck into his shirt collar as a napkin?

22 Q: What does Huggy use for candlelight?

23 Q: From what does he hang the lantern?

24 Q: To whom does Starsky propose a toast?

ANSWERS

SEASON ONE

1.0 "Pilot"

1 A: *Red River.*

2 A: Frankie's Gym.

3 A: Coffee and a Danish.

4 A: Hutch's.

5 A: Shells, Starsky's Beretta, Hutch's .38, flares (6) tear gas grenades (4), shotgun, radios (2), flashlight, and "the book."

6 A: Zebra Three.

7 A: 1600 hours.

8 A: Cindy and "What's-Her-Name."

9 A: Coley.

10 A: 058 AZT.

11 A: A bar.

12 A: It was written in ink from the pen Hutch loaned him.

13 A: A pool table.

14 A: Lakers vs. Knicks.

15 A: Six.

16 A: 849 ASB.

17 A: Black.

18 A: Nancy.

19 A: A steam room.

20 A: 58.

21 A: Rainstorm.

22 A: Tiger.

23 A: Hutch.

24 A: Starsky.

25 A: "Mayday!"

26 A: An adult movie theatre.

27 A: A Thermos.

28 A: Defensive back.

29 A: The fire escape.

30 A: Brown.

31 A: The seventh.

32 A: The roof of his car.

33 A: Sweeping the stairs.

34 A: "Trust me."

1.1 "Savage Sunday"

1 A: The funnies.

2 A: A bow tie.

3 A: 50.

4 A: Pink.

5 A: Starsky.

6 A: "Three bucks."

7 A: Green.

8 A: A pencil.

9 A: 1963.

10 A: Capt. Dobey.

11 A: 5:00

12 A: It gives the place a bad name.

13 A: Hot dogs.

14 A: He throws it out.

15 A: $50

16 A: Monty's Bar.

17 A: Pretzels.

18 A: One of the Gran Torino's tires.

19 A: Ohio.

20 A: 500.

21 A: A hamburger.

22 A: 555-6673.

23 A: A motorcycle.

24 A: Starsky.

25 A: "Get him the hell out of here!"

26 A: A toll booth.

27 A: The Lakers.

28 A: Huggy Bear.

1.2 "Texas Longhorn"

1 A: The glass slipper.

2 A: Hutch.

3 A: A snow tire.

4 A: His tie.

5 A: $15.

6 A: A cigarette.

7 A: He kicks it and yells at it in Spanish.

8 A: "Mean" Joe Greene.

9 A: Blue.

10 A: A comic book.

11 A: His left.

12 A: The silver boot tip.

13 A: A folder.

14 A: 33240.

15 A: Drinking money.

16 A: A vending machine.

17 A: Starsky's.

18 A: A scorpion and a frog.

19 A: Huggy Bear.

1.3 "Death Ride"

1 A: $360.

2 A: Black.

3 A: Southern Memorial.

4 A: *You Bet Your Treasure.*

5 A: The left.

6 A: "I'd rather worry."

7 A: "Me and thee."

8 A: Hutch.

9 A: Two.

10 A: George.

11 A: "Squeeze!"

12 A: His watch.

13 A: Starsky.

14 A: A rock.

15 A: Boots.

16 A: Ice-cold lemonade.

17 A: Marcus Welby.

18 A: "Of course it hurts."

19 A: *Pong.*

1.4 "Snowstorm"

1 A: Three.

2 A: Dalmatian.

3 A: He's tired.

4 A: Two.

5 A: $100.000.

6 A: Four million dollars.

7 A: Dobey.

8 A: Under the floorboards.

9 A: A car lot.

10 A: "A striped tomato."

11 A: Through the window.

12 A: The ocean.

13 A: Hutch.

14 A: Dobey.

15 A: Elmo Jackson.

16 A: One.

17 A: Capt. Dobey.

18 A: Five.

1.5 "The Fix"

1 A: A dime.

2 A: He gives it a kick.

3 A: Love.

4 A: Starsky.

5 A: Pinball.

6 A: Hutch's gun.

7 A: Seaview Point.

8 A: $50.

9 A: Huggy's.

10 A: A coffee cup.

11 A: Checkers.

12 A: Coffee and candy.

13 A: The left.

14 A: A cab.

15 A: "You want to drive my car?"

1.6 "Death Notice"

1 A: Ginger.

2 A: "Ginger will die tonight."

3 A: Southern.

4 A: Headphones.

5 A: His left.

6 A: Manny.

7 A: Hutch.

8 A: Starsky.

9 A: Ollie (Oliver Hardy.)

10 A: Starsky.

11 A: "Only when I can't see down."

12 A: Starsky.

13 A: A pencil.

14 A: The phone.

15 A: Repairing them.

16 A: Arnold's.

17 A: Milk.

18 A: Neon.

19 A: A car.

20 A: A waterfall.

21 A: "Black Bean Soup."

22 A: Huggy Bear.

23 A: "Love for good friends, gratitude for their helping, and prayers for all the good things in the future."

1.7 "Pariah"

1 A: A slice of pizza.

2 A: A blender.

3 A: Hutch.

4 A: Hutch.

5 A: His tie.

6 A: Three.

7 A: "Thanks."

8 A: "Hi, guys."

9 A: Hutch.

10 A: Two.

11 A: Starsky.

12 A: 3A.

13 A: Hutch.

14 A: "The old zoo."

15 A: Hutch.

16 A: A daiquiri.

1.8 "Kill Huggy Bear"

1 A: Baker Six and Zebra Three.

2 A: Hutch.

3 A: Popcorn.

4 A: His girlfriend, Sarah's.

5 A: Candy apple red.

6 A: Playing pinball.

7 A: He makes the machine tilt.

8 A: Hutch's.

9 A: Carrot juice.

10 A: Time.

11 A: Hutch.

12 A: Vitamin E and wheat germ.

13 A: "Stuff it."

14 A: Which one of them should jump out.

15 A: Carrot juice.

1.9 "The Bait"

1 A: The instep.

2 A: Two.

3 A: His shoes.

4 A: Dobey's.

5 A: The Hawaiian Missionary, 1859.

6 A: Wonton soup.

7 A: Jimi Hendrix.

8 A: Milk.

9 A: Four weeks.

10 A: By turning on the clock radio.

11 A: 10:00.

12 A: Starsky.

13 A: A forklift.

14 A: Cheryl.

15 A: Green.

16 A: "Mother McCree's Kosher Cure-All."

1.10 "Lady Blue"

1 A: 20 minutes.

2 A: Sneaky Pete.

3 A: "Weimaraner Four."

4 A: The Mellow Yellow.

5 A: A photo of herself and Helen.

6 A: Waveform energy.

7 A: His calculator.

8 A: Aluminum foil.

9 A: Coffee.

10 A: Hutch.

11 A: His pocket watch.

12 A: It stinks.

13 A: All the buttons are pro-grammed to the same station.

14 A: The butt of his gun.

15 A: Green.

16 A: Alpha Centauri.

17 A: Starsky.

18 A: He called Starsky's mother.

19 A: "Eat your vegetables."

1.11 "Captain Dobey, You're Dead!"

1 A: *Madame Olga's Self-Help Program to Become Right-Handed.*

2 A: To the candy machine.

3 A: Starsky and Hutch.

4 A: His daughter, Rosie.

5 A: Herself.

6 A: Rosie and Cal's bikes.

7 A: Starsky and Hutch.

8 A: *The Maxie Malone Show.*

9 A: Chess.

10 A: Edith.

11 A: Starsky.

12 A: A baseball glove.

13 A: More milk.

14 A: On a box on his desk.

15 A: Capt. Dobey.

16 A: *Twister.*

17 A: Rosie's.

18 A: His tie.

19 A: Rosie.

1.12 "Terror on the Docks"

1 A: The aisle.

2 A: Starsky.

3 A: Margaret.

4 A: Hutch.

5 A: Vincent Price.

6 A: It opens by itself.

7 A: Organ music begins to play.

8 A: The unique way he folds his gum wrappers.

9 A: He makes Hutch's skin crawl.

10 A: She slaps him.

11 A: A bottle of Castor oil.

12 A: "The devil."

13 A: Hutch.

14 A: "A prospective son-in-law."

15 A: Hutch.

1.13 "The Deadly Imposter"

1 A: David.

2 A: The locker room.

3 A: Five years.

4 A: The Corsican Brothers.

5 A: A knife.

6 A: A mako shark.

7 A: "Husky and Starch."

8 A: S.O.S.

9 A: A cannon.

10 A: Turner Beach.

11 A: 537 ONN.

12 A: The ones he hasn't been paid to kill.

13 A: His handcuffs.

14 A: Abigail Crabtree.

1.14 "The Shootout"

1 A: Starsky.

2 A: A chair.

3 A: "Lagoosi."

4 A: Bulls vs. Stags.

5 A: Midnight.

6 A: Beer.

7 A: Joey.

8 A: The vino de casa.

9 A: Two.

10 A: A tablecloth.

11 A: Capt. Dobey.

12 A: Vic Monte.

13 A: Sammy and Robin.

14 A: His watch.

15 A: The shoulder.

16 A: "Years."

17 A: Chicken soup.

18 A: "I love you."

19 A: Camille.

20 A: She upends a serving tray.

21 A: Michael.

22 A: The Sammy Grovner School of Hilarious Humor.

23 A: His left.

1.15 "The Hostages"

1 A: 7:00.

2 A: Ames.

3 A: Starsky.

4 A: Chicago.

5 A: Every 45 minutes.

6 A: Starsky.

7 A: An encyclopedia salesman.

8 A: A plumber.

9 A: A motorcycle/minibike.

10 A: Hutch.

11 A: "Sweet Hutch."

12 A: Field work.

13 A: Yram is Mary backwards.

14 A: "Good afternoon, Belle."

15 A: Starsky.

16 A: A pound.

17 A: 517.

18 A: Hutch.

19 A: Ten bucks.

1.16 "Losing Streak"

1 A: Hutch.

2 A: Hamburgers.

3 A: "Autumn Leaves."

4 A: One sees E, the other sees B.

5 A: *Vic Rankin Plays the Blues.*

6 A: Pink.

7 A: Teddy bear.

8 A: Twelve years.

9 A: Ziggy's Jazz Café.

10 A: A dog.

11 A: "Queen of the May."

12 A: The hairs on the back of the neck curl up.

13 A: "No, they haven't."

14 A: Having his shoes shined.

15 A: On the street.

16 A: The stage.

17 A: Hutch.

1.17 "Silence"

1 A: Hutch.

2 A: Starsky.

3 A: A candy bar.

4 A: His jeans.

5 A: The bonnet.

6 A: Kittens.

7 A: Matthew 7:15.

8 A: Eating.

9 A: Starsky.

10 A: Six hours.

11 A: Holmes and Watson.

12 A: A train store.

13 A: 71.

14 A: Marty.

15 A: Popcorn.

16 A: Two of the kittens.

17 A: It relives itself on him.

1.18 "Omaha Tiger"

1 A: Fireball.

2 A: The Olympic Auditorium.

3 A: A flying drop kick.

4 A: Three.

5 A: "Yeah."

6 A: Full Nelson and Half Nelson.

7 A: She felt Starsky's gun.

8 A: One of the ropes.

9 A: DePew's Meat Packing Company.

10 A: Rodent Downs.

11 A: He starts calculating how much time they have left before they run out of air.

12 A: 165.

13 A: Red.

14 A: Eddie.

15 A: He kisses him on both cheeks.

1.19 "JoJo"

1 A: "All bloody morning."

2 A: "Federal Space Rangers."

3 A: Folding a paper airplane.

4 A: The horn goes off.

5 A: He shows her his badge.

6 A: Karate.

7 A: Cleaning the backseat of Hutch's car.

8 A: Milk.

9 A: They glow in the dark.

10 A: Earl's Custom Car Cult and Body Shop.

11 A: "That red tomato with the white stripe."

12 A: A pizza box.

13 A: Rodin.

14 A: The trunk opens.

1.20 "Running"

1 A: Ducks.

2 A: Four.

3 A: A box of nails.

4 A: Capt. Dobey's.

5 A: *To Sharman from Tony.*

6 A: Sharman's room key.

7 A: 27.

8 A: Two.

9 A: He throws it against a wall.

10 A: Woodshop.

11 A: 2000 Ridgeway Ave.

12 A: Hutch.

13 A: He drives away.

14 A: Playing his guitar.

15 A: Starsky and Hutch.

1.21 "A Coffin for Starsky"

1 A: Hutch.

2 A: His pants.

3 A: Travel agent.

4 A: Dave.

5 A: Sweating.

6 A: Sweet Alice.

7 A: Her gum.

8 A: A camera lens.

9 A: Blue.

10 A: Starsky.

11 A: Capt. Dobey.

12 A: A cane.

13 A: A cup of water.

1.22 "Bounty Hunter"

1 A: Crocodiles.

2 A: Butterfly bones.

3 A: Happily married.

4 A: Lola.

5 A: Hutch.

6 A: He was left by aliens to spy on humans.

7 A: *Werewolf by Night.*

8 A: An apple.

9 A: "Starchy and Hup."

10 A: Hutch.

11 A: The corner of Marshall and Chandler.

12 A: Starsky.

13 A: Vitamin E.

SEASON TWO

2.1 "The Las Vegas Strangler, Part 1"

1 A: Slamming his office door with his foot.

2 A: "About 1946."

3 A: Hutch.

4 A: A slot machine.

5 A: "Vegas fever."

6 A: Hutch.

7 A: 17 black.

8 A: Craps.

9 A: Starsky.

10 A: Hutch.

11 A: Most Likely to Succeed.

12 A: Starsky.

13 A: Seven.

14 A: He's blushing.

15 A: Starsky.

16 A: Scotch.

17 A: Four in the morning.

2.2 "The Las Vegas Strangler, Part 2"

1 A: Starsky.

2 A: Four.

3 A: Hutch.

4 A: His brain.

5 A: Iris.

6 A: Hutch.

7 A: Circus Circus.

8 A: Her barking dog.

9 A: Starsky.

10 A: Starsky.

11 A: Hutch.

12 A: Vicky and her daughter.

13 A: Keno.

2.3 "Murder at Sea, Part 1"

1 A: Sir Winston.

2 A: Hearts and spiders.

3 A: Duluth, Minnesota.

4 A: telescope.

5 A: A magic shop.

6 A: Hutch.

7 A: A torpedo tube.

8 A: A bow tie.

9 A: *Amapola.*

10 A: Simon Says.

11 A: Looking for things on a scavenger hunt list.

12 A: Playing "Greensleeves" on the zither.

13 A: Tuppleman.

14 A: "My Wild Irish Rose."

15 A: "Popeye the Sailor Man."

16 A: Nicky Cairo.

17 A: First Officer Stafford.

2.4 "Murder at Sea, Part 2"

1 A: Reading.

2 A: Hutch.

3 A: At least half.

4 A: Six.

5 A: "I don't know."

6 A: Hutch.

7 A: Starsky.

8 A: Hutch.

9 A: Stafford.

10 A: Huggy Bear.

2.5 "Gillian"

1 A: Starsky.

2 A: Starsky.

3 A: The hood.

4 A: Pepper.

5 A: A shark tooth.

6 A: Hard candy.

7 A: Huggy Bear.

8 A: $1600.

9 A: Her apartment, her car, and her safe deposit box.

10 A: Hutch.

11 A: Venice Place.

12 A: Starsky.

13 A: Al.

14 A: 24.

15 A: Starsky.

16 A: He punches Starsky.

17 A: A fire hose.

18 A: "A bingo."

19 A: Red.

20 A: An infield fly.

2.6 "Bust Amboy"

1 A: A hearse.

2 A: A walkie talkie.

3 A: A coffin.

4 A: Hutch.

5 A: His hat size.

6 A: 17.

7 A: The needle marks on her arm.

8 A: Flypaper.

9 A: Peanut butter burritos con jelly.

10 A: The *London Daily Dispatch*.

11 A: Caviar.

12 A: Darts.

13 A: In Huggy's foot.

14 A: A bumblebee.

15 A: Thirty-five cents.

16 A: A cosmetics company for men.

2.7 "The Vampire"

1 A: Red.

2 A: A cape.

3 A: The Play Pen.

4 A: Huggy's cousin Louie.

5 A: Popcorn.

6 A: The phone's handset cord.

7 A: Beanbag chairs.

8 A: Starsky.

9 A: Ballet.

10 A: Cedar.

11 A: A clove of garlic.

12 A: A Complete Vampire Protection Kit.

13 A: 25.

14 A: Over 200.

15 A: Hutch.

16 A: Goat's blood.

17 A: Starsky.

18 A: Dancing.

19 A: On the bureau.

20 A: Plastic vampire teeth.

2.8 "The Specialist"

1 A: Brushing his hair.

2 A: Two.

3 A: He shaves off his moustache and colors his hair.

4 A: The Chapel of Bodily Invigoration.

5 A: His desk.

6 A: Baers Plumbing.

7 A: 39.

8 A: Reading the Bible.

9 A: "Mr. Personality."

10 A: Sally.

11 A: Medium rare.

12 A: The oil fields.

13 A: For leaving her tied up in the oil fields, and for laughing at her in the restaurant.

2.9 "Tap Dancing Her Way Right Back into Your Hearts"

1 A: A rose.

2 A: "Flaunt it."

3 A: He pops an inflated paper bag.

4 A: The doorman.

5 A: Argentina.

6 A: $25,000.

7 A: Mouse o' War.

8 A: $30,000.

9 A: A tow truck.

10 A: Two.

11 A: Hutch.

12 A: A forklift.

13 A: Hutch.

2.10 "Vendetta"

1 A: Flowers.

2 A: 1964.

3 A: A bare lightbulb.

4 A: Jingo.

5 A: Starsky.

6 A: He says, "Hello, plants."

7 A: A dead rat.

8 A: The Yankees and the Chi-Sox.

9 A: .247.

10 A: Every time he drives around a block.

11 A: He ate it.

12 A: JFK half dollars.

13 A: Starsky.

14 A: Sunglasses.

15 A: "Shave and a Haircut."

16 A: Starsky.

17 A: Hutch.

18 A: Norwegian.

19 A: Baseball cards.

2.11 "Nightmare"

1 A: 21 years.

2 A: Uncle Elmo's

3 A: Running on foot.

4 A: Starsky's clothes.

5 A: A towel.

6 A: A train set.

7 A: They end up broke.

8 A: Huggy's Ark.

9 A: Sam the Greek.

10 A: A paper cup.

12 A: Starsky.

13 A: A train set.

14 A: A puppy.

2.12 "Iron Mike"

1 A: Bowling league.

2 A: His feet.

3 A: Capt. Dobey.

4 A: Coyle Provision Company.

5 A: JFK.

6 A: His hat.

7 A: Hutch on Starsky's.

8 A: Wyatt Earp.

9 A: 555-7263.

10 A: Jersey City.

11 A: "Give a little, get a lot."

12 A: A motorcycle.

13 A: Cocaine.

14 A: Chess.

15 A: "Talk a little, win a lot."

2.13 "Little Girl Lost"

1 A: On her right.

2 A: Christmas.

3 A: A reindeer.

4 A: Nothing.

5 A: A Star of David.

6 A: 560 South Main.

7 A: "We Wish You a Merry Christmas."

8 A: Two.

9 A: Salami.

10 A: A Christmas tree.

11 A: Flowers.

12 A: The fights.

13 A: A priest.

14 A: "Donder, Blitzkrieg, Spritzen."

15 A: Kiko.

16 A: Playing piano.

17 A: An Army/Navy Surplus Store.

18 A: Mrs. Ramos.

19 A: Hutch.

20 A: Her baseball glove.

21 A: An ant farm.

22 A: Kiko.

23 A: A new caboose for his train set.

24 A: A tree planted in his honor.

2.14 "Bloodbath"

1 A: The courthouse steps.

2 A: A parade float from Mars.

3 A: He goes to the restroom.

4 A: "Where is Starsky?"

5 A: "Starsky."

6 A: While he's awake.

7 A: "At the ending."

8 A: Dirt.

9 A: 11.

10 A: Starsky's badge and ID.

11 A: A bull.

12 A: A hooded robe.

13 A: A bear.

14 A: Huggy Bear.

15 A: Huggy.

16 A: "Don't thank me."

17 A: "Garbage belongs with garbage."

18 A: The interior.

2.15 "The Psychic"

1 A: Fireball.

2 A: Hutch.

3 A: The straw.

4 A: Atlantic City.

5 A: Two.

6 A: "Grazing in the sun."

7 A: Hutch.

8 A: A handkerchief.

9 A: Rosa's Tamales.

10 A: The Turbos.

11 A: Starsky.

12 A: Hutch.

13 A: 211.

14 A: Hutch.

15 A: Green and Kawasaki.

16 A: Boots.

17 A: Don's Arcade.

18 A: 90 seconds.

19 A: Blue.

20 A: A Laundromat.

21 A: A minute.

22 A: "Captain Surreal."

23 A: A bar and grill.

24 A: 30 seconds.

25 A: Three.

26 A: Moo-Moo.

27 A: "Lazarus."

28 A: A scarf.

29 A: Hutch.

30 A: "Huggarino the Magnificent."

31 A: "I'm pickles, he's onions."

2.16 "The Set-Up, Part 1"

1 A: Casa Madrid.

2 A: Two.

3 A: "Patty!"

4 A: Two weeks.

5 A: City Cab Company.

6 A: "The Puce Goose."

7 A: "The Blonde Blintz."

8 A: Under his hat.

9 A: About seven years.

10 A: Joe Durniak.

11 A: Half a dozen.

12 A: Joe.

13 A: "Here lies Joe Durniak, the end of an era."

14 A: A bowling alley.

15 A: 906.

16 A: Our Lady of Sorrows.

17 A: Hutch.

18 A: Debra.

2.17 "The Set-Up, Part 2"

1 A: Every 30 seconds.

2 A: Hutch.

3 A: A piece of material he left behind on a coat hanger.

4 A: A time bomb.

5 A: Starsky's apartment.

6 A: A bowling ball.

7 A: He pinches Thistleman's nose.

8 A: Desert Springs.

9 A: N63230.

10 A: Terry.

11 A: A corned beef on rye.

12 A: Hutch.

13 A: Hutch.

14 A: A framed picture of who Terry knows as his late wife.

15 A: Two.

16 A: Terry.

17 A: "The African chap with the arsenal."

2.18 "Survival"

1 A: A desk lamp.

2 A: Capt. Dobey.

3 A: His left.

4 A: A Mercedes.

5 A: Two.

6 A: "Where?"

7 A: An ice pack.

8 A: The Dynamic Duo.

9 A: He cuts himself.

10 A: Barnaby's Tavern.

11 A: "Battle Hymn of the Republic."

12 A: Occupied France.

13 A: A piano.

14 A: Her hand.

15 A: The Hotel Garvey.

16 A: Mildred.

17 A: The fifth sector.

18 A: 16.

19 A: Condemned c. 1847.

20 A: "It's beautiful."

2.19 "Starsky's Lady"

1 A: Basketball.

2 A: Hutch.

3 A: 612.

4 A: Huggy Bear.

5 A: His thumb.

6 A: Roses.

7 A: Skating roller derby.

8 A: Starsky.

9 A: 32.

10 A: Hutch.

11 A: *Monopoly.*

12 A: Yellow.

13 A: Quit the force.

14 A: Red.

15 A: The slides.

16 A: She asks who won the basketball game.

17 A: Hutch.

18 A: The kitchen.

19 A: The Vancouver Lions.

20 A: The utilities.

21 A: Midnight.

22 A: A book — *A Thousand Ways to Win Monopoly*.

23 A: Her Teddy bear.

24 A: Ollie.

2.20 "Huggy and the Turkey"

1 A: Starsky.

2 A: The Pits.

3 A: Darts.

4 A: Brown.

5 A: The spirit world.

6 A: A Cadillac.

7 A: Brazil.

8 A: A water heater.

9 A: He whistles.

10 A: He throws a bus bench through their windshield.

11 A: They fake a fight.

12 A: Hairstylists.

13 A: Farrah Fawcett.

14 A: A comb.

15 A: Tyrone.

16 A: Mr. Marlene.

17 A: Apples.

18 A: The water heater.

19 A: His left.

20 A: "Tennis, anyone?"

21 A: An 1854 Golden Eagle.

22 A: $3,000.

2.21 "The Committee"

1 A: An Adopt-a-Rock.

2 A: Bumper pool

3 A: It bit her.

4 A: Starsky.

5 A: Moon Café.

6 A: A tuna burger with lots of mushrooms.

7 A: Capt. Dobey.

8 A: The dentist.

9 A: Starsky.

10 A: Four.

11 A: Two.

12 A: An apple.

13 A: Her house.

14 A: "The Original Centurian."

15 A: His rock.

16 A: The Medal of Valor.

2.22 "The Velvet Jungle"

1 A: Starsky and Hutch.

2 A: Two.

3 A: Hutch.

4 A: Starsky.

5 A: "Who's dead?"

6 A: "Starchy."

7 A: Hutch.

8 A: Guitars.

9 A: Broken glass from her window falling in front of them.

10 A: Two.

11 A: The fountain.

12 A: Charlie Chaplin.

13 A: A guitar.

14 A: Hutch.

15 A: Because a red one might clash with his tie.

9 A: Huggy Bear.

10 A: Mantle and Maris, respectively.

11 A: Third.

12 A: The Adams Hotel.

13 A: 311.

14 A: Imperial.

15 A: Hutch.

16 A: Starsky's.

17 A: Starsky.

18 A: Hutch.

19 A: The Singing Policeman.

20 A: The Blonde Blintz.

21 A: He trips.

22 A: "Lovin' Arms."

2.23 "Long Walk Down a Short Dirt Road"

1 A: The Saddle-Bar Club.

2 A: A tent.

3 A: $10,000.

4 A: Hutch.

5 A: Capt. Dobey.

6 A: A truck.

7 A: "Wrap Your Love All Around Your Man."

8 A: He was stabbed in the throat.

2.24 "Murder on Stage 17"

1 A: A water deliveryman.

2 A: Three and a half.

3 A: Monarch Studios.

4 A: The Wolf Pack.

5 A: Kate Jackson.

6 A: Red.

7 A: Spaghetti and Meatballs.

8 A: He trips.

9 A: Hutch.

10 A: "Here comes McCoy now."

11 A: Sierra Springs.

12 A: Starsky.

13 A: Mustard.

14 A: Starsky.

15 A: Tea.

16 A: Western.

17 A: *High Noon.*

18 A: *Honeymoon for One.*

19 A: Starsky.

20 A: Chaplin.

21 A: 11.

22 A: Sunglasses, trench coat, and a hat.

23 A: His mom.

24 A: Starsky.

2.25 "Starsky and Hutch Are Guilty"

1 A: At Dobey's desk.

2 A: A knife.

3 A: Juggling oranges.

4 A: Building a model car.

5 A: 27 years.

6 A: Fifi.

7 A: Charlie Brown.

8 A: Starsky.

9 A: A matchstick.

10 A: The Wildcat League.

11 A: Hutch.

12 A: Judith Coppet's.

13 A: He bleaches his hair and parts it on the wrong side.

14 A: "Blueberry Hill."

15 A: Six.

16 A: His tennis racket.

SEASON THREE

3.1 "Starsky and Hutch on Voodoo Island"

1 A: The Jungle Club.

2 A: Bigfoot.

3 A: Checkerboard.

4 A: Flight 19.

5 A: Fort Knox.

6 A: Starsky.

7 A: Red.

8 A: Huggy Bear.

9 A: Two.

10 A: One.

11 A: The 9th.

12 A: The left.

13 A: Two.

14 A: Softly.

15 A: Starsky.

16 A: Janice.

17 A: Charlotte.

18 A: Hutch.

19 A: Whichever side the boar is on.

20 A: Hutch.

21 A: Starsky.

22 A: Hutch.

23 A: Four.

24 A: $10,000.

25 A: It flies out of her hand due to Starsky's driving.

26 A: Thorne's wheelchair.

27 A: Huggy and Godfrey.

28 A: *Rodan Meets Godzilla.*

29 A: A feather from Papa Theodore's belongings.

3.2 "Fatal Charm"

1 A: Hutch.

2 A: Hutch.

3 A: His right.

4 A: A bullet for him to bite on.

5 A: A vending machine.

6 A: Over his front door.

7 A: Spaghetti.

8 A: That she was Hutch's kid sister from Boston.

9 A: A watch.

10 A: *Forever, Diana.*

11 A: He draws his gun.

12 A: "Damn."

13 A: Building a model ship.

14 A: Starsky.

15 A: He has to follow where the cord leads.

16 A: Huggy Bear.

17 A: Starsky.

18 A: Ketchup.

19 A: Flowers.

20 A: $800.

3.3 "I Love You, Rosie Malone"

1 A: Jogging.

2 A: Eagles.

3 A: Dr. J (Julius Erving.)

4 A: In Dobey's office.

5 A: Goodson's.

6 A: "Have a nice day."

7 A: Mozart.

8 A: A dentist.

9 A: White.

10 A: Hutch.

11 A: "I should have taken a longer breath."

12 A: Freshly squeezed orange juice.

13 A: Chambers.

14 A: That Shelby will inherit it.

15 A: In the car.

16 A: He runs, faster and faster.

17 A: Hormones.

18 A: A three-day-old burrito.

3.4 "Murder Ward"

1 A: Starsky.

2 A: "Somewhere Over the Rainbow."

3 A: Hutch.

4 A: One week.

5 A: Jane Hutton.

6 A: He pulls it out from under him.

7 A: Five-card stud.

8 A: A basketball.

9 A: Starsky.

10 A: The First Annual Cabrillo Cockroach Derby.

11 A: The Cabrillo Kid.

12 A: A straw and a Ping Pong paddle.

13 A: Sunglasses.

14 A: *The Big Sleep* and *The Long Goodbye*.

15 A: A blue Chrysler.

16 A: Hutch.

17 A: Freddie's.

18 A: His apple.

19 A: Nurse Bycroft.

20 A: Starsky.

21 A: Two.

22 A: He pushes a laundry cart in his way.

23 A: "Happy Birthday."

24 A: A nurse.

25 A: Diana Stiles, R.N.

26 A: Babe Ruth's.

3.5 "Death in a Different Place"

1 A: Ten.

2 A: Three.

3 A: The Green Parrot.

4 A: 305.

5 A: An electric fan.

6 A: The St. Francis.

7 A: Hutch's.

8 A: He says he inherited it.

9 A: A gold medallion.

10 A: Custard.

11 A: 101.

12 A: Shaving.

13 A: A mirror.

14 A: Sugar.

15 A: Hutch.

16 A: A piano.

17 A: The bar.

18 A: Six.

19 A: Huggy Bear.

20 A: Hutch.

21 A: Hutch's.

22 A: The back seat.

3.6 "The Crying Child"

1 A: Stan Laurel and Oliver Hardy.

2 A: The Los Angeles Dodgers.

3 A: He waxes it.

4 A: Lake Tahoe.

5 A: She's a part-time book-keeper.

6 A: A sushi chef and go-kart mechanic.

7 A: Hutch.

3.7 "The Heroes"

1 A: A newspaper.

2 A: A cigar.

3 A: Flies.

4 A: A tape recorder.

5 A: An aspirin.

6 A: He spills it on Larry.

7 A: Scorpio.

8 A: Two.

9 A: Mutt and Jeff.

10 A: Starsky.

11 A: "The Heroes."

12 A: Tear it down.

13 A: *"Where?"*

14 A: A door.

15 A: He falls through it.

3.8 "The Plague, Part 1"

1 A: 140.

2 A: Starsky.

3 A: 11:00.

4 A: A suitcase.

5 A: It gets towed.

6 A: Blue.

7 A: A writer.

8 A: The locker room.

9 A: Hutch.

10 A: A newsstand.

11 A: The firing pin.

12 A: $5,000.

13 A: The trunk.

14 A: A transient.

15 A: Army.

16 A: A buck.

17 A: His shoes.

18 A: Six.

19 A: Hutch.

20 A: 48.

21 A: Two.

22 A: "Limousine service."

23 A: Starsky.

3.9 "The Plague, Part 2"

1 A: His upper lip.

2 A: Movie magazines.

3 A: His car.

4 A: A lipstick.

5 A: "Starsk."

6 A: 12 years.

7 A: His gun.

8 A: Captain Marvel.

9 A: Dr. Meredith.

10 A: Chess.

11 A: Three.

12 A: Flowers.

13 A: 555-4598.

14 A: The airport and the hospital.

15 A: $100.

16 A: A tree.

17 A: Helen.

18 A: The big leagues.

3.10 "The Collector"

1 A: Scoot Jackson.

2 A: Red.

3 A: Kill.

4 A: One.

5 A: Walk on it.

6 A: Guns.

7 A: Under her bed.

8 A: He blows it up.

9 A: Six.

10 A: The Pits.

11 A: Acrophobia/a fear of heights.

12 A: His liquor license.

13 A: A leg of lamb.

14 A: Hutch.

15 A: Cane.

16 A: Hutch.

17 A: A suitcase.

18 A: Ground beef.

19 A: A stuffed animal.

20 A: One.

21 A: His ankles.

22 A: Hutch.

23 A: He asked a cop to help find it.

24 A: It was eaten by alligators.

25 A: Mayonnaise.

3.11 "Manchild on the Streets"

1 A: Basketball.

2 A: Jackson.

3 A: He's a bus driver.

4 A: Starsky.

5 A: The rear bumper.

6 A: Apple 304.

7 A: Mrs. Fellers.

8 A: A beer.

9 A: Keys.

10 A: Patient and orderly, respectively.

3.12 "The Action"

1 A: Marlborough Health Club.

2 A: Football.

3 A: Clipping.

4 A: His mouth.

5 A: Hutch.

6 A: $1,000.

7 A: Salty Babe.

8 A: Second Place.

9 A: Josie the N.

10 A: Tony.

11 A: An ice cube.

12 A: The Professor.

13 A: Starsky.

14 A: Hutch.

15 A: Starsky.

16 A: His mortgage and his wife.

17 A: Liar's poker.

18 A: His money.

3.13 "The Heavyweight"

1 A: The couch.

2 A: Tony Zale.

3 A: Booker Wayne.

4 A: The third.

5 A: Hutch.

6 A: Honolulu.

7 A: The Dolphin Hotel.

8 A: Jeeter.

9 A: $5,000.

10 A: Booker.

11 A: Starsky.

12 A: Oregon.

13 A: She's engaged.

14 A: He spills it in Hutch's lap.

3.14 "A Body Worth Guarding"

1 A: The Kirov Ballet.

2 A: Muhammad Ali.

3 A: "Brava!"

4 A: Starsky.

5 A: The sight.

6 A: That she loves to talk about herself.

7 A: Walking on their hands.

8 A: A snowbank.

9 A: Arm wrestling.

10 A: Licorice.

11 A: *"Tadzhik."*

12 A: "Mr. Starrefsky."

13 A: "Hootch."

14 A: "I Wish I Was."

15 A: The key isn't over the door.

16 A: Two.

17 A: Kaufman.

18 A: Arm wrestling.

3.15 "The Trap"

1 A: The Yamamoto Reflex.

2 A: 29.

3 A: A shopping cart.

4 A: A florist.

5 A: Hutch.

6 A: Hutch.

7 A: A cigarette lighter.

8 A: The floor of the back seat.

9 A: The back of the passenger seat.

10 A: Two hours.

11 A: *The Great Escape.*

12 A: Charles Bronson.

13 A: His leg.

14 A: Hutch's.

15 A: A Model T.

16 A: Kerosene.

17 A: His watch.

18 A: Joey.

19 A: Dobey.

3.16 "Satan's Witches"

1 A: Hutch's.

2 A: Red.

3 A: Pine Lake.

4 A: A boot.

5 A: Starsky.

6 A: Face-down on a bar.

7 A: The refrigerator.

8 A: Starsky.

9 A: "Mad Merlin."

10 A: A tree.

11 A: "Hi!"

12 A: Blind Man's Bluff.

13 A: "Cha-cha, or tango?"

14 A: A telephone.

15 A: Fishing.

16 A: The roar of a bear.

3.17 "Class in Crime"

1 A: Her hand.

2 A: The scope.

3 A: Hutch.

4 A: *The Rookies.*

5 A: "Polish it."

6 A: Mickie.

7 A: Rhetorical.

8 A: Mickie.

9 A: Jack and Allen.

10 A: "Get a warrant, call my lawyer, and rock and roll."

11 A: Their clout.

12 A: He'll bend down to pick up a seashell.

13 A: A year.

14 A: Starsky.

3.18 "Hutchinson for Murder One"

1 A: The Pits.

2 A: A cigarette.

3 A: A Brandy Alexander.

4 A: Under the passenger seat of Hutch's car.

5 A: Brandy.

6 A: B -.

7 A: Starsky.

8 A: Dryden.

9 A: Starsky.

10 A: A table.

11 A: He unloads it.

12 A: A mortuary.

13 A: A coffin.

14 A: Huggy.

15 A: $250.

16 A: A guinea pig.

3.19 "Foxy Lady"

1 A: A slice of pizza.

2 A: Hutch's snoring.

3 A: He slams the front door.

4 A: The note from Lisa.

5 A: In Hutch's mouth.

6 A: Algiers.

7 A: $100.

8 A: A bag of groceries.

9 A: The left.

10 A: Lisa.

11 A: An airplane.

12 A: His dirty laundry.

13 A: $50,000.

14 A: Her suitcase full of clothes.

3.20 "Partners"

1 A: Springtime.

2 A: Throw up.

3 A: A pickup truck.

4 A: *"Hutch!"*

5 A: "Starky."

6 A: Pinochle.

7 A: "Dopey."

8 A: If he's the Chief of Police.

9 A: Lewis and Clark.

10 A: Dr. Bear.

11 A: Terry.

12 A: *Monopoly.*

13 A: Traffic control.

14 A: Their whistles.

3.21 "Quadromania"

1 A: A set of bolt cutters.

2 A: Chess.

3 A: *Macbeth.*

4 A: A banana.

5 A: A guitar.

6 A: Third and Main.

7 A: Checkers.

8 A: A pillow.

9 A: In a trunk.

10 A: An old lady.

11 A: Three.

12 A: KC.

13 A: KC.

14 A: Huggy Bear.

3.22 "Deckwatch"

1 A: A .38.

2 A: His leg.

3 A: His lighter.

4 A: A quart.

5 A: Harry.

6 A: One hour.

7 A: His leg.

8 A: Hazel.

9 A: Blood.

10 A: Three.

11 A: Lemon meringue.

12 A: Starsky.

SEASON FOUR

4.1 "Discomania"

1 A: *Intimidation: Controlling People for Love and Money.*

2 A: Tostadas.

3 A: Eight feet.

4 A: Marty.

5 A: Starsky and Hutch.

6 A: Hutch.

7 A: Starsky.

8 A: Red.

9 A: Hutch.

10 A: The salsa samba.

11 A: Hutch.

4.2 "The Game"

1 A: "Gray hair and more wrinkles."

2 A: Two.

3 A: Hutch.

4 A: Every two hours.

5 A: The Hotel Californian.

6 A: Huggy Bear.

7 A: Dobey.

8 A: Three.

9 A: Ernie Silvers.

10 A: Godzilla.

11 A: Gina.

12 A: His coffee table.

4.3 "Blindfold"

1 A: A blowtorch.

2 A: 2%.

3 A: Dobey.

4 A: A camera.

5 A: Greta Garbo.

6 A: A trumpet.

7 A: Pool.

8 A: "Thank you."

9 A: Hawaii.

10 A: Each other.

11 A: Starsky.

12 A: Starsky.

13 A: Emily.

14 A: Days.

15 A: Three.

16 A: The vacuum cleaner.

4.4 "Photo Finish"

1 A: *The Lounge Lizard Monthly.*

2 A: The back of the jacket rips.

3 A: One.

4 A: A mouse.

5 A: A toy police car.

6 A: $10,000.

7 A: Headphones.

8 A: Boris.

9 A: Backgammon.

10 A: Basil Monk.

11 A: Behind the grandfather clock.

12 A: The White Witch.

13 A: Six.

14 A: Starsky.

15 A: Hutch.

16 A: Their tuxedos.

17 A: Champagne.

18 A: The price tag.

19 A: Starsky.

4.5 "Moonshine"

1 A: Wood grain alcohol.

2 A: Eliot Ness.

3 A: Twenty.

4 A: Yellow.

5 A: Alabama.

6 A: Starsky.

7 A: He rips it up.

8 A: His feet.

9 A: C.W. Jackson.

10 A: "Oh, my gears."

11 A: The Backwoods Inn.

12 A: Johnny Stovall.

13 A: Bell County.

14 A: 25.

15 A: Hutch.

16 A: The left.

17 A: The still.

18 A: Hutch.

19 A: The foxtrot.

4.6 "Strange Justice"

1 A: $15.

2 A: Disco.

3 A: Her sandwich.

4 A: 39.

5 A: O'Reilly.

6 A: A gun.

7 A: The Baltimore Hotel.

8 A: 204.

9 A: Stand-up comedian.

10 A: Hutch.

11 A: Capt. Dobey.

12 A: "Why is Slate doing all the talking?"

13 A: Starsky.

14 A: Hutch.

15 A: Starsky.

4.7 "The Avenger"

1 A: A week.

2 A: Hutch.

3 A: An astrological biorhythm calculator.

4 A: Tea.

5 A: Arm wrestling.

6 A: 211.

7 A: The Cellar.

8 A: Self-defense.

9 A: A guitar.

10 A: Bobbie.

11 A: The telephone.

12 A: Bobbie.

13 A: "You!"

14 A: Brown.

15 A: Triple-zero.

16 A: The palm of his hand.

4.8 "Dandruff"

1 A: Mr. Marlene.

2 A: French.

3 A: Mr. Tyrone.

4 A: In the hotel's fountain.

5 A: Starsky.

6 A: The Belvedere Diamonds.

7 A: His choice of cigars.

8 A: A magazine.

9 A: His stepladder.

10 A: Leo.

11 A: Superba Corona Superbas.

12 A: $175.00.

13 A: The stepladder.

14 A: Six.

15 A: Gold.

16 A: A flower.

17 A: A box.

18 A: Sixteen.

19 A: A police officer.

20 A: In his hat.

21 A: Pedicures.

22 A: The Baron

4.9 "Black and Blue"

1 A: His ESP quotient.

2 A: Blue.

3 A: Seven.

4 A: Blue Seven.

5 A: A bird bath stand.

6 A: Two.

7 A: Soup.

8 A: Cigarettes.

9 A: Her gun.

10 A: The overhead lamp.

11 A: $100.

12 A: Starsky.

13 A: His hat.

14 A: A banana.

15 A: Save the world.

16 A: Bruce.

17 A: His blue eye would give him away.

18 A: His TV.

19 A: His left.

20 A: Dobey.

21 A: Hutch.

22 A: "What are you gonna do?"

4.10 "The Groupie"

1 A: One.

2 A: Switzer Protection.

3 A: *Vogue*.

4 A: A cruise ship.

5 A: Milk.

6 A: Lilacs and roses.

7 A: Fosdick.

8 A: Class of '65.

9 A: 800.

10 A: Two bucks.

11 A: Roy Sears.

12 A: James Bond.

13 A: "Jacques Penney."

14 A: 19.

15 A: The swimming pool.

16 A: Melinda.

17 A: Starsky.

4.11 "Cover Girl"

1 A: A donut.

2 A: The dentist.

3 A: An airplane.

4 A: Two.

5 A: Chess.

6 A: Seven.

7 A: Everything.

8 A: Hutch is Turkey Buzzard, Starsky is Chicken Little.

9 A: Hutch's.

10 A: Walter Allen.

11 A: Pillows.

12 A: Minnie.

13 A: A postal letter carrier.

14 A: A seashell.

15 A: Starsky.

16 A: Hutch.

17 A: Starsky and Hutch.

18 A: Anger.

4.12 "Starsky's Brother"

1 A: "I love you."

2 A: Mrs. Krupp's baseball bat.

3 A: It's getting ticketed.

4 A: Nicholas Marvin Starsky.

5 A: The Velvet Slide.

6 A: Nick.

7 A: "I'm a Loser."

8 A: The couch.

9 A: Rubble from the explosion.

10 A: Four.

11 A: Love.

12 A: He forgot his wallet at The Pits.

13 A: Carmelle Printing.

14 A: Hutch.

15 A: $10.

16 A: $20.

17 A: Left.

4.13 "The Golden Angel"

1 A: His right.

2 A: Block, Block, Harvey, and Block.

3 A: Four.

4 A: Howard Cosell.

5 A: "Curly."

6 A: The Slam.

7 A: "Die Saturday night."

8 A: His halo.

9 A: A stool.

10 A: Three.

11 A: A harp.

12 A: Brass knuckles.

13 A: Lying on the mat, watching.

14 A: Camille's wig and sunglasses.

15 A: Starsky.

16 A: Pacifist.

17 A: Nine bucks.

18 A: January 16th, 1979 (which is this episode's original air date.)

4.14 "Ballad for a Blue Lady"

1 A: Hutch.

2 A: A cocktail napkin.

3 A: "Perch a blue butterfly on a velvet apple."

4 A: Nashville.

5 A: Billie Holiday and Bessie Smith.

6 A: Her sheet music.

7 A: His badge/ID.

8 A: Marianne.

9 A: Her life.

10 A: One.

11 A: Hutch's greenhouse.

12 A: Three.

13 A: Donna Summer.

4.15 "Birds of a Feather"

1 A: The St. Francis.

2 A: 307.

3 A: Seven.

4 A: Luke's tie.

5 A: "Mr. Huggy."

6 A: Three queens/three of a kind.

7 A: The radio and the TV.

8 A: He burns it.

9 A: Starsky and Hutch.

10 A: An attaché case.

11 A: To her sister's.

12 A: $50,000.

13 A: Three.

14 A: Luke.

15 A: Capt. Dobey.

16 A: The Southside Stickman.

17 A: Eight ball in the corner pocket.

18 A: He scratches, losing the game.

4.16 "Ninety Pounds of Trouble"

1 A: Hutch.

2 A: He hurts his foot.

3 A: The Cordon Bleu Room.

4 A: He's looking for his wallet.

5 A: A strawberry margarita.

6 A: Flipping playing cards into his hat.

7 A: A syringe.

8 A: "Love and kisses from Schiller."

9 A: Joey.

10 A: Bruce Springsteen.

4.17 "Huggy Can't Go Home"

1 A: Muhammad Ali

2 A: Milk.

3 A: Bagels.

4 A: Cream cheese.

5 A: Aces.

6 A: Two.

7 A: Playing pinball.

8 A: The Funky Chicken.

9 A: The Belmont.

10 A: On the hood of his car.

11 A: A broken bottle.

12 A: Big Red.

13 A: A pipe.

14 A: "A long way from home."

15 A: The Pits.

16 A: His beer.

4.18 "Targets Without a Badge, Part 1"

1 A: Las Vegas.

2 A: A toothbrush.

3 A: The jack of hearts.

4 A: The peace sign.

5 A: A pinwheel.

6 A: A pay toilet.

7 A: He flashes the headlights on his car twice.

8 A: Hutch.

9 A: 1041.

10 A: Mardean's sister.

11 A: Mardean.

12 A: The supermarket.

13 A: Huggy.

14 A: Jamie.

15 A: The pinwheel from Lionel's drumkit.

16 A: They throw their badges into the ocean.

4.19 "Targets Without a Badge, Part 2"

1 A: A can.

2 A: An umbrella.

3 A: Belle.

4 A: Hutch's hat.

5 A: A car door.

6 A: In a car crash.

7 A: Flower Power.

8 A: "Really? Try mine."

9 A: The engine.

10 A: O'Reilly.

11 A: The permit for them to carry guns.

12 A: "Staying alive, captain."

4.20 "Targets Without a Badge, Part 3"

1 A: White on white.

2 A: The steam room.

3 A: They're sprayed down by a street cleaner truck.

4 A: A cowboy hat.

5 A: "Furry."

6 A: A wrecking ball.

7 A: "Why you instead of me?"

8 A: 48th Street.

9 A: Huggy Bear.

10 A: They exchange them with one another.

4.21 "Starsky vs. Hutch"

1 A: Sherlock Holmes.

2 A: Susan.

3 A: Minnie.

4 A: Re-assembling a rifle.

5 A: The couch.

6 A: One month.

7 A: "THE SPY WILL DYE."

8 A: Decorative plates.

9 A: Pool.

10 A: 1646701.

11 A: A newspaper.

12 A: Hutch.

13 A: The Golden Lady Ballroom.

14 A: Backgammon.

15 A: Starsky.

16 A: A daiquiri.

4.22 "Sweet Revenge"

1 A: A necklace.

2 A: Ping Pong.

3 A: Starsky.

4 A: Six.

5 A: Huggy.

6 A: Huggy.

7 A: Capt. Dobey's.

8 A: A Ping Pong ball.

9 A: Reading a book.

10 A: *The Thinker.*

11 A: Gunther.

12 A: Bates.

13 A: The arrest warrant and his handcuffs.

14 A: One.

15 A: 8:45.

16 A: Four

17 A: He puts it on his head.

18 A: A bottle of Jim Beam.

19 A: A ten-pound antipasto.

20 A: A bottle of wine.

21 A: The plastic wrap from the antipasto.

22 A: A lantern.

23 A: The ceiling's water sprinkler.

24 A: "Four very heavy dudes."